12/21/21

To Father Va [barcode: D1189667]

Wishing you all
the best in the flow of life!

With Love,

Maureen McGargill & Lana
Carpenter

The Current

Poems for the Flow of Life

Connie Burnett Cruthirds

The Current/Connie Cruthirds - 1st ed.

Hardback ISBN: 979-8-9850650-0-8

Mom, your words were heard.
This one is for you.

Art, Skyler, and Adam,
You are beloved.

Contents

Part Three: Self Portrait

P.S.

Preface

I've become an early riser. In this still time before the rest of the house awakes, I open my journal, light a candle, connect with my breath, and slowly become aware of all around and within me. On most days, words begin to flow that I often don't remember writing.

Three years ago, I'd lost my way in a world of too much and never enough.

Since I was a little girl, life often felt too big for me. I preferred to live in my imagination. These truths helped me perfect an eating disorder, become a people pleaser, live in fear, and follow "the rules" as perfectly as possible. Throughout the decades of my life, much healing and progress had been made in many areas, but I often still listened to the bad ideas the addictive and compulsive parts of me offered as relief.

By April 2018, I had no access to my creativity. That scared me more than any other diagnoses or realties I was facing. With no access to my imagination and creative spirit, death seemed just one breath away. Desperate, I asked for help. Then I got honest and sober in my actions and behaviors. I learned to love my human self as is and let spirit lead me forward.

This collection of poetry was written for you and for me. There are no poems in this book that I intentionally sat down to write. In the morning's stillness and throughout the day, I listen and narrate what I see and hear. Sometimes the words feel like they are tapping me on the shoulder. I've learned that I either stop and let them flow onto the page or they float away. The more I become willing to drop in deeply, way beneath my ego, the faster the words flow.

Writing has helped me remember who I truly am as: a playful soul bravely doing this human gig.

Several months ago my dear friend and fellow writer, Melissa Faber, got my attention when she suggested I publish a book of poetry. I was pretty determined to focus on novel writing, but alas, she was right.

As I began to sort through hundreds of poems, I realized the stack I kept focusing on was labeled "current". I researched the word current in my dictionary and thesaurus and clearly saw the three-fold connection to these poems: the words, like the flow of life, surge like an electrical current illuminating and energizing, or stream like the Mississippi River rushing outside my writing window, plus these poems emerge from present life circumstances.

I compiled this collection like a puzzle. I trusted the pieces would show me where they fit and that a picture would emerge. Once the puzzle was complete there appeared a three part book.

As you journey through *The Current*, the arc of a story will unfold-
   Part One "The Earth and Her Moon" is both beautiful and humbling as
   I bear witness to the vast universe and the majesty of earth -its delights,
   teachers, and longings.

   Part Two "Life" paints a picture of living through life's challenges,
   realizations, inspirations, and possibilities.

Part Three "Self Portrait" offers a more intimate look into an individual's personal path to becoming more alive.

I offer to you with great joy *The Current: Poems for the Flow of Life*.

P.S. With the manuscript almost complete, I met with my brilliant artist friend Hannah Kate Lewellen, owner of HKate Art & Design. She had earlier agreed to format and add basic black and white designs to my book and submit it to printing. I talked to her about how much I'd love to see the poems illustrated. Hannah said she could make that happen and she really did. Hiring Hannah to illustrate The Current and working with her has been expansive and magical. Some of the drawings are her response to the poems as she read them. Many are her interpretation of conversations we had about what I was experiencing at the time. I can't thank Hannah enough for her beautiful, inspired artistry.

All Life

Last night I dreamed we dined again
beside the Adriatic,
near the canals of Venice.
The sea tossed.
Our youth matched her wildness.

Yesterday my friend asked
if I knew that Jewish tradition celebrates
four new years every year.
Each season brings the invite
to begin again again.

The Chinese medicine man
shook his head at New Year's day resolutions
doomed to high percentage fail.
He said our body is designed to follow the seasons.
It's winter, our inner soil needs rest.
Plant your resolve come spring.

Scientists discovered a tiny new species,
A nano-chameleon living in Madagascar,
the size of a sunflower seed,
smallest reptile on earth.
Just one male. Just one female.
Called B. Nana. Nana for short.

One a dream.
One a revelation.
One a truth.
One soon to be critically endangered.
All life.

Part One: The Earth and Her Moon

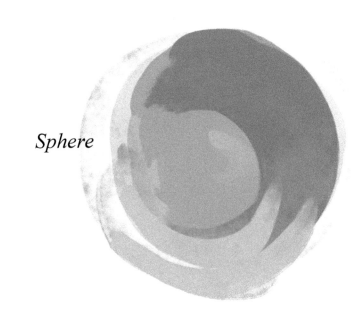

Sphere

Sphere

This sphere we ride on
rotates at the exact rate needed
to paint the seasons,
stun us with eclipses,
and keep us from falling off.

This sphere we ride on
with its raucous hot bubbling center,
tectonic plates jostling for position,
and mountain building rebel heart
slowly shows her majesty one layer of life at a time.

She stuns us
to awaken us
from this deep sleep
of vacillation between control and out of control.

Earth,
her billions year old self,
tells a story about
our silliness,
our righteousness,
our huff and puff as if the house is ours to blow down,

but it's not.

So let's sit
for one minute
and ponder the brilliance of it all
until we realize
that
we
are
just
too
small
to ever really get it.

Perhaps,
but we can
shine humbly,
ride this sphere
as she spins on her axis,
and
respect that only together
will we revolve around the sun
again.

The All of This

The creaking of the woods before deer appear.

I'm waiting.
Patient.
Still.
Sensing.
Early morning stirred us awake
to feast upon the majesty of this sky.

Suddenly it changes.
Gray turns to blue,
slowly paints its edges a salmon color words cannot capture.
Geese honk their joy
as the early bird naps,
full from worms already devoured.

How did the moon sneak over me so quickly?
How does the crow not weep over the beauty of what unfolds
above and around in this dome of the sky?

And just like that,
it's as if Michelangelo reached through the heavens
and changed the palette again
to keep me awake and in awe.

The all of this is so much more than our narrow focus sees.

Pink yields to yellow blending into white
as I breathe it all in more deeply.

Soon the day will take off in a hurry towards something.
Something that might separate me
from this dome that holds the sky
whispering everything I most need to know.

Walden's Heart
Part One: The Human's Perspective

Flat,
heart shaped grey stone
rested on the shore.

Lifted by kind hands,
the heart
was again tossed
into Walden Pond.

This rock didn't skip.
This rock landed
and sank.

Ripples refract light
split by surfaces cracked.

Like a fresh born baby,
surface breaking is sharp
and
worth a worthy bellowing.

Part Two: Grey Stone Heart's Perspective

Resting,
I got to say I was there
beside Walden Pond,
telling the stories from way back then
when I was rough and jagged.

Back then
before
water flowed over me.
Moved quickly across my skin,
Exfoliating what wasn't meant to stay.
Eventually, I was stripped too bare.
Fracturing,
sediment came,
filled my deepest cracks
made me whole again
just before I might have
broken
in two,
or three.

Resting on the shore,
I told stories of yesterday's hero's sagas
that seemed heroic enough
until suddenly, minutes ago,
I was tossed back in the game.

Dang.
That shore was cozy.

I knew
the arc of the sun,
the paws of prowlers,
the tails of beavers,
the skin of hot summer's slithering snakes,
the first pelt of a fat, full raindrop,
the tickle of full moon's fairy dance at midnight.
You know,
magic.

Now my view is skewed.
Murky.
Light beams reach through surface.
I long to grab one,
be pulled back to shore.
Instead,
I sink
and
look around
as what's around looks at me.

A keen eyed turtle,
neck stretched long,
pokes me with her pointed nose.
Her little one nuzzles to bite,
but my shell is harder than hers.
Their friends swim over,
check out my raucous landing,
see me settle,
and glide on by.

Tossed back in,
I begin to remember
the warm hand that

picked me up,
held me tight.
She looked at me,
slid her finger around my smoothed edges,
noticed the slight dip in the top of me and smiled.
With a sigh,
held deep
and
long enough to birth butterflies,
her words floated up from her breath
out into the air
"My heart".

Together we stepped to water's edge.
Her hand clasped around me
rose to her mouth.
She filled a single wish
with her longings
and
whispered it to me between her palms.

Just before she opened her palm out flat
she picked me up between her fingers,
and touched me to her lips
before tossing
me back into the water.

Wish holder,
   wish willed,
      wish launched,
         wished well,
            wish well intended.

Part Three: A Wish for You

To you, the wishing whisperer,
may your jagged edges be smoothed,
may what's no longer needed be released,
may rich sediment fill your cracked places,
until another wish maker entrusts you with their longings
and you believe they will come true.

Shadows

Lavender skies are on the rise.

Moon lights dawn's sky
before she yields to sun's light.
Sun, she shines fully
behind clouds in her way.
Her rays reach through,
touching this and that
to remind me,
she is here.

Branches lit by streetlights
cast mystical etchings on
manmade concrete.

Shadows surround me.

Lavender blends with blue-grey
as bare trees hold nothing back.
Their static shadows
stand firm in this windless sky.

I see me there in their outlines.
My shadow is stagnant, too.
I wander lost between closed doors
of what was
and
what wants to be.
I know this place
like a tornado closet's refuge.
It almost fools me into
believing I can stay here.

Slammed against rocks and shores,
Rough waves rolled us for so long.
Their rhythm seeped into my
blood and called itself life.

This snare of stillness feels like a trap.
Tension grips my knees, freezes my feet,
while a million unlocked doors
to possibility surround me.

Tears rise as stark shadows
hold firm in winter's light
wondering like me,
"Where did the coverings that shaded me,
the birds that entertained me go?"

This place is asking for something
that I have yet to meet within me.

As I wonder if it exists,
a single sun ray
shifts shadow's etchings.

In the Soil of My Soul

I can't go back and clean it all up.

Begin here
in this moment
and move forward
incrementally through
sedimentary layers
painting my years.

The Grand Canyon of my life
formed
when tears flowed,
outer winds blew,
inner earthquakes shook,
yet
there,
here,
I am.

In the past week
my view has changed.
Tips of leaves on bare branches
pushed through wood.
Slowly, daily,
they've opened wider,
brand new,
bright spring green.

In the canyon of my life
a new layer forms.

This layer
has been a tougher one.
Fighting the winds,
denying the truth
is exhausting until surrendered,
I let go
and
flow
returns
again.

Layers, leaves, the return of two bikers
before the dawn.

Life.

I'll just leave this here,
step back,
watch to see colors emerge,
patterns reveal,
as this new layer forms
in the soil of my soul.

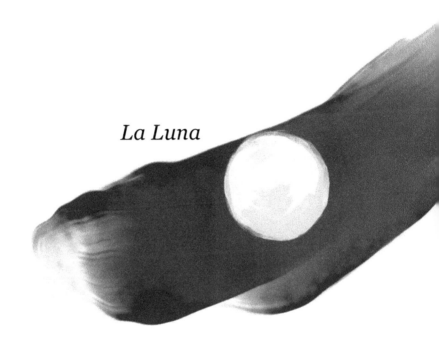

La Luna

Crush

I have a crush on the moon.

Day or night
when I see her
high or low
I smile.

From deep within me,
something rises up
and cheers for her.

Her seasonal path,
her white presence on blue sky background,
her catching my wandering attention throughout the month
as she grows
from sliver to fully embracing the light around her.

On some of my darkest days,
seeing La Luna
reminds me of my place in this universe.

I, too, wax and wane.
My moods,
my forgetting what matters most,
my doubting what can be,
my getting lost in day's happenings.

On this cold December morning,
I wake early to meet this page,
meditate my mind,
exercise my muscles,
so I can return to my heart.

The moment I open my shutter
I see her,
just above the tree in front of me,
almost completely full of light,
yet
slightly shrouded in clouds.

I smile.

She knows what words cannot capture,
what my truth won't admit,
what my soul holds close to heart.

That's why I so love this moon.

Now,
the radiance of her light expanded well beyond her sphere,
she begins to slide behind barren trees.

I bow my head to her in gratitude
and
sweetly tuck the gift of this love
into the center of my heart.

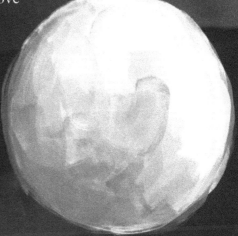

Darkness

Darkness,
so black I can barely see the trees.
I'm startled,
by what might be right in front of me.

Electricity stopped.
Big boom, pop.
Daylight not yet here.

La Luna,
my moon,
my crush,
where are you?

Eyes adjusted,
fear subsides,
I look for you.

Our urban jungle dimmed,
your stars shine brighter now.

Their twinkle bolder
without interference from all we've made.

The sun will rise.
Until then,
I'll sit in the dark,
and remember to be a light, like you, in this world.

The Arc of the Moon Obfuscated

Blurred,
I squint to see
if that is you.

Between
me
and
you,
there are clouds,
thin,
fast,
undefined,
keeping me from
fully
seeing you.

In this house,
I sometimes feel small,
confined.

In your house,
even within spacious space,
do
you
ever long to leave,
break free from your arc,
take a break
from all of us
watching you
as you wax and wane?

Moon do you yearn
to step away
for just a day
and not be you?

Day woke me harsh.
Night dream's villain
revealed
life's truth.

Anger glared.

My body not knowing
sleep from awake.

My pricked spirit
cast me adrift
until
cold hardwood
connected
my bed warm feet
with today.

This day's beginning,
first tarnished
by my startled psyche,
relaxed
once my opened shutter
revealed you, my moon.

"Obfuscated."
That's what I heard as you greeted me,
"I'm obfuscated."

Yes, you were.
I was, too.

You, blurred by clouds.
Me, blurred by life.

Mirrored.
I sat and stared.

Companions.
Still.
Breathing.

Morning's sun came.
Clarity came, too.

Drop the Reins

Hello again, Moon.

Today, you show me your left half
at first bright against cerulean sky,
now lighter as night pales,
and softens its blue to baby.

On the surface of you,
I see dark patterns,
background white.
I'm mesmerized.
Wanting nothing else now,
but to be lost in curiosity about you.

The steadiness of you on your axis,
phases predictable and powerful.
Seas rise and fall in response to you.
Slivers of you intrigue my eyes.
Your monthly fullness
lights paths I might have missed.

Me, often scattered, preferably untamed,
I humbly surrender
the catch in my breath,
the hesitancy of my steps,
when you catch my eye,
at just the right time.

For you I am grateful.

Now, in these last minutes,
before you fade into sun's background
and new day launches into action,
I notice flock after flock of birds flying between us.

Me stilled,
eyes on you,
breath softens.
I settle in deeper,
and drop the reins
I'd planned to harness on this day.

Instead, I notice
the increasing volume of morning's chirps,
winds arriving to escort in later rain,
the click then clack of a nearby train's
wheels rolling south towards New Orleans,
another sharp shrill rises from a bird I cannot see.

Within all of this, I know I am home.

Interrupted

I thought I'd missed you moon.

Power out, I woke early
surprised to see your light
high above downtown's darkness.

What a sight!
You almost,
but not quite,
full of yourself
shining in the clear night sky.
Alone,
powerful,
seemingly still,
but ever so slightly
inching away.

Me?
I returned to bed.

Nightmares.
Bad wedding bands
interrupting silent retreats.

Waking to the tinkling of a gentle alarm
interrupted by the sharp sound
of a too early text
filled with harsh words
of didn't you know
or did you do.

I did what I've learned to do,
find you.

You, now a softer white,
against dawn's cornflower blue sky.
You too quickly slipping behind the rooftop between us.
You who watches over me and comforts my soul.
Please help me make sense of this world when it spins too fast.

Moon,
before the last sliver of the top of you
gives way to sun's rising,
I bow and send a piece of my heart with you.

Slide Into Lilac Skies

Moon, I see you peeking at me.
Thought you'd packed it up for the day.

Soon you'll slide into lilac skies,
bounce down through wintering trees
like a white shot pinball.

Will you float across the Mississippi river?
Notice the seeds of sunflowers sleeping
'til summer heat teases them out?

Do you move through your months
from whole to sliver and back again
aware of the power you have
over me and the seas?

Suspended now upon a pale blue sky,
your light dims.

How good it is to know
you're always there
bringing flow to my ebbs
and ebbs to my flow.

Muddied Water

Moon's shadow fading,
dawn turns into day.

My heart steadied,
I feel her beat again.
Rapid then slow.

Four birds fly up
circle the sky around moon
and scatter.

See, that's the thing about all of this.
Some days might look like muddied water,
but underneath,
Life.

Storms roll over me.
Lightning snaps me in two.

But is that true?

Mind hijacked.
Conclusions made.
Until suddenly still,
I notice the birds have gone silent
and know
there's been too much made
of this heavy moment in my life.

Put it down,
for now just put it down,
make space to breathe.

This house, too small for all it holds.
I fling open the doors,
crank open the windows,
and leave before moon's shadow takes her rest.

Creature Guides

Why Are We Here?

Why are we here?

Whatever it is,
it is everything.

The bird chirps morning sounds
with no response
but just to sing.
Deeper warbles vibrate close
from distant trees,
But it's her shrill
that harkens the morning
awake.

My candle flickers
with urgency
then suddenly still.

My morning question
"Why are we here?".

Today in this now of my life.
I'm here to learn to notice
that one bird's voice
stirring this 5am silence.
The single small plane
flying over vibrating the
glass heart hanging on my window.

I'm here to notice raindrops
on that window from last
night's storm still here

to reflect street lights
until sun brightens this majesty.

Yesterday I was here
to see the spider hanging in her
web within the bridge
above the broad Mississippi River
and wonder what that view of
the world looked like to her.

I'm here to feel the delight
offered by a coy crocus.
She teased me for days with
her subtle opening and closing.
Then when she was ready
she fully revealed her petite grandeur,
in vibrant purple, neon orange,
lemon yellow, and crisp white.
For that second she took my
breath away and tucked it
into her purpose of being.

I'm here to immerse myself in that moment
when a new spring ladybug
smoothly landed on my hand.
She explored each finger
from top to bottom until
her wings silently lifted her,
landing on my other hand
again exploring each finger.

When finished,
she paused,
at the tip of one finger,
looked at me
for quite awhile,
and
flew back towards
the river.

Simplistic.
Yes.
Until the sun soon rises
and
I speed off into my scheduled life
soon to need to remember again

The Relevance of Our Irrelevance

It's all so much bigger than
our capacity to comprehend.
Each of us here
to further a piece of something
greater than what's imaginable.

We are at once important
and also minuscule.

In the palmetto field
behind my sister's house
lives a broad shouldered bobcat
who shares the land

with

bunnies,
ears aware,
freely frequenting
their favorite spots,

an owl that flies from perch to perch
to view what crawls on earth below,

and

mice that swiftly move between plants
in search of plump insects to chomp.

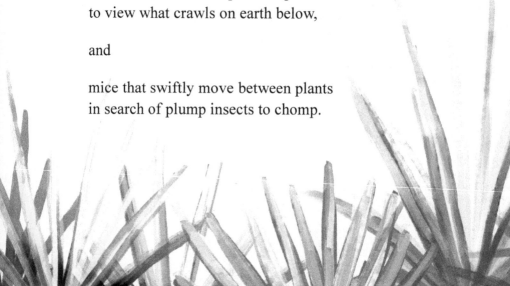

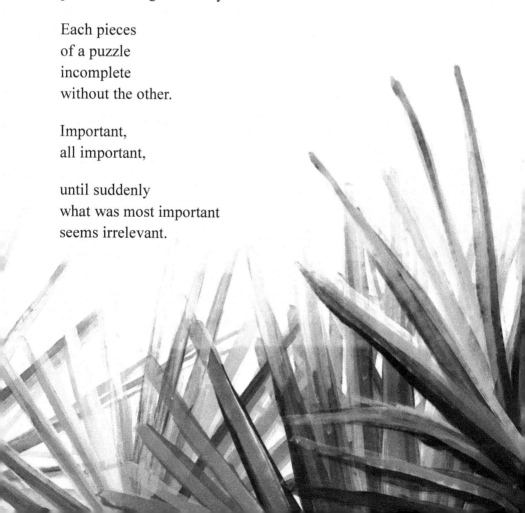

Wind blows around them on this sunny day.
Hunger stirs within them.
Instinct aims them towards each other.

Voracious needs
vital for vitality,
become
vittles for sustainability.

All important
as life circles
and
pulls our being into many roles.

Each pieces
of a puzzle
incomplete
without the other.

Important,
all important,

until suddenly
what was most important
seems irrelevant.

Simple but Divine

Oh to fly like a bird
choose any tree
and look down from above

Oh to balance on limbs
as wild winds toss
my being from side to side

Oh to take off swiftly
dive briskly
and watch my shadow follow along

Oh to find broken sticks
weave tight a nest
to warmly nestle my young

Oh to sing out
from daybreak to dusk
symphonies of warbles
lasting just for this moment

Oh to see nature so close
respond to instinct
and surrender to season's call

Oh to be like a bird
just being a bird
simple but divine

Soaring on waves
of mystery
in ways words just can't describe

The Land Knows Her Truth

As the sun begins to rise over the mountains,
I watch for dark night's
foxes,
bears,
and mountain lions
to cross the open fields on their way to day's shelter.

Tired from a night of feeding and mischief,
their bellies just almost full enough
to satiate their wildness
yet leave them hungry for more.

I sit here in this window seat
humbled by this land.

Instinctively,
I see my place
in the hierarchy of time.

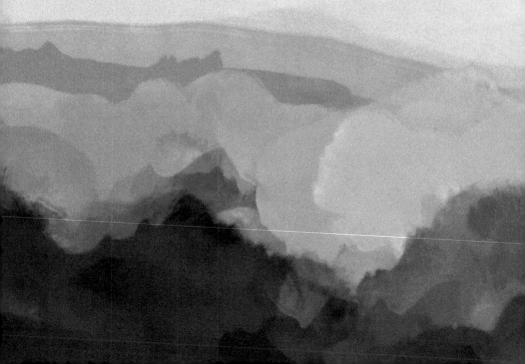

We,
plus
the
foxes,
bears,
and
mountain lions,
are brief dwellers
in this beauty
waking up around me.

Deep in the rumblings of her underbelly,
the land knows her truth.

She looks at me with kindness,
slightly shaking her head as if to say,
"Now there, there my child.
No need to speak for this land.
Just rest yourself upon my chest
and feel what stirs within."

With gratitude,
I take myself closer to her,
and
rest my cheek upon her heart.
Soon my erratic breaths change,
as her ancient beats revive my rhythm.

The Beauty of the Stall

Flying into the wind,
I hover.
Pensive. Instinctive.
Seemingly stalled to you, my observer.

Fascinated,
I move closer to you
there on the dock
longing to fly.

Watch me to see
what stalled can do.

She puts her pen down.
Pauses her narration.
Looks up at me as I glide
from over head to out in front.

I show her steady.
I show her focus.
I show her the beauty of the stall,
the gift of stillness
though my wings never stop their steady motion.

My eyes fixed upon my prey below,
I pause to look back at my observer,
slightly tipping my beak
to bring her fully into our moment.

I send a shake of motion
from the center of my being
to my wings.
Ready, I pull them inward
until I see my prey more clearly.
Head aimed up, then sharply down.
I dive headfirst,
aware my observer thinks
she knows the rest of this story.

To keep her awake,
I teach her more about the finesse of the stall.

Suddenly,
I reverse my momentum,
shifting my dive
from beak to talons down,
fiercely piercing the sea,
grasping my dinner like fish caught in a boat's net.

Smoothly, I rise
never releasing contact
with her mesmerized eyes.

I end our lesson with one sharp cry
filled with all she needs to remember.
"Fly my sweet,
for what you seek
is waiting just below the surface."

Pray not Prey

I heard my Mother whisper my name.
Her presence gone now almost 15 years.

I'm in a hermitage, in the middle of a woods,
retreating from a world of too much and not enough.

Rain pours upon this little place.
A flock of geese fly over
honking this new day's awakening.
They're the ones that always make me feel
like my Mother is still close by.

I am filled with delight
as morning's light
slowly touches this place.

Still tired, my eyes began to close again
when sharply I heard her say my name.

Just last week,
I tried to remember her voice.
I talked about how long it's been
since the breath of life filled
her sweet little ballerina body.

She didn't want me to miss this morning
where sun rises behind thick clouds

filled with rain overflowing
onto trees surrounding me.

Light makes its way through clouds,
as trees still barren from winter's chill
glisten with drops of rain
spilling over their branches.

Last night I stilled myself on a porch
as dusk held light's curtain slightly open.

Just below seven deer grazed
keenly aware I'm there, too.

They'd dine upon the brush
then pause to look up at me.

Humbled,
I lowered my face to show
I am here to pray not prey.

More stilled,
my heart rate slowed,
my breath softened,
my love for this moment
grew sweetly from my soul.

Joy,
the kind that radiates,
that rides on winds unseen,
rose within me
when one after another
the deer came closer.

Their mouths nibbling day's offering.
Their eyes lifting and lowering watching mine.

Dusk darkened,
I remained still
until one by one
they looked up at me
and gracefully exited stage left.

Filled,
their bellies and my heart,
the loneliness that brought me here,
let go.

Of Bumbling Bees and Bells

Mourning dove's coos,
ooh, wah, ooh, ooh, ooh,
each spaced evenly apart.

I hold my breath listening for her next verse.

Three little dogs chase a young squirrel.
Quickly he scurries to the first low branch.
Wraps his arms around it and stills his scurry.

Early morning yesterday,
two fat bees bumped and parted
into each other
as they flew around crêpe myrtle blossoms
ripe for fat bee sucking.

The dove's verses grow further apart.
I can't hold my breath
to unknown songs and rhythms I'm still learning.

The sun begins to rise behind me.
Violet skies surrender to light's palette
as she adds a little pale pink to the foreground.

Me, here above ground in my little treehouse of an office,
I watch days move through their rhythm
without resistance visible to me.

Train wheels screech against steel rails in the distance.
Car gears shift from slow to fast just around the corner.
A single plane flies over shaking us a little
as air parts to its power.

Sky painting continues
as white lightens to blue.

Resting birds begin to fly,
but the bees aren't yet awake.
I don't know where these bees,
I've come to know so well, sleep.
I do know they don't come
to feast upon their puffy white blossoms
until night surrenders to light
so they can better see their buffet of discernment.

Last year, on a downtown Chicago street,
I stilled myself by a planter flourishing with flowers.
I watched a single bee lift itself up,
Wings moving almost imperceptibly
from blossom to blossom,
walking the edge of each flower,
discerning her desire,
until she found exactly what she wanted.
When found she dove in headfirst
like an Acapulco cliff diver waiting
for that perfect water rise.
This bee, so discerning, so determined,
so aware as senses shifted flight
to find the flower that bloomed
just for her to taste
its sweetest nectar.

Lost in memory,
I'm startled back to this day's awakening
by the Basu bell on my meditation timer
telling me I need to move on to what's next.

But, I like it here
where
the sky goes from deep indigo
to a cotton candy swirl of blue and pink,
where
the rhythm of the dove paces my breath,
where
the biking couple appears at 5:52am
their lights shining,
their clothes matching,
their words indistinguishable floating up
between the verses of the dove.

Like a child called in from play,
I surrender to what's next.

Street lights still glowing,
bees not yet awake for breakfast,
I reach to put on my shoes,
climb onto my stationary bike,
and dream about what nature might teach me next.

Nature Guides

Slow to Rise, Easy to Fall

Lately,
I've been
slow to rise
easy to fall.

Early bird sings,
no interest in worms.

Yesterday,
I looked inside
a soft pink azalea blossom.
five continuous petals.
Nature painted one
with a deep pink design.
Each flower the same
except for a rogue branch
on that bush,
covered in hot pink flowers.

Today,
I think about this world
where spring blooms
are painted so perfectly.
Beautiful irises rise from a tough winter's dirt,
birds hurry to rebuild or reclaim nests for their young,
guilty people defend their wayward actions,
innocent people defend their wrong convictions,
political hatchets split family trees,
while a little baby tenaciously lives
with a half of a heart in backwards.

I know so little
about the vastness of it all.
Yet, I sense the delicate pattern on the azalea petal,
the rise of the sturdy purple iris,
the continual song of morning birds
hold clues much overlooked.

When I'm long gone,
    the dramas of the day ceased,
    the delight of the last petal examined fades,
    the curiosity of the why of it all dims,
    the baby, the birds, the flowers
    their aliveness will linger.

May the backdrop of life
move into the foreground of my path
to better show me the way forward.

What Does the Tree Feel?

I want to write a poem about you.
Your bare winter branches
pondering blossoms and spring,
glistening before me now.
Dripping in nature's icy bling,
your sparkling beauty up lit
by glazed street lamps.

What I see is so beautiful.
What you feel must be heavy
as your limbs bow,
offered without choice
to all that falls upon you.

In the wee hours,
thunder and lightning
stomped around us.
Startled me awake
to check on you.

You who I sit with daily,
watch leaves come and go.
squirrels play upon you,
bees explore you,
birds chirp our mornings
loudly into being.

In this moment,
you show me your truth.

Though life is happening,
your branches precariously heavy,
you stand firm,
radiating the light
of who you are,
present to this moment
trusting within you,
spring has already sprung.

Sprung

Spring is springing!
Yesterday's bare limbs,
today's little sprouts of hope.

Bare winters,
especially ones like this one
plagued by endurance,
send me looking for spring.

Yesterday, I passed a redbud tree,
tall, slick dark branches.
This morning?
Bare no more!
My eyes leap for joy,
open wider.

I see pert little fuchsia buds,
natures' painted beauties,
now cover yesterday's barren branches.
I look up as a single cherry tree waves,
"Me too!"

Awakening?
Could be.
Remembering?
Yes.
The tree knows it's time
to let go of this long wintering.

Strike Me Wild

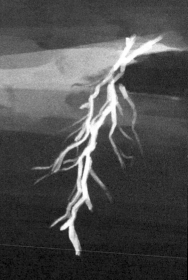

Lightning strikes
strike me wild
on this dark March morning.
Narrating your antics,
I feel you
the air, the temperature
the wind, the rain
spinning your self into a tizzy.

600 strikes per hour.
My aren't you feisty.

You shake our house.
Rattle our windows.
Rumbling out one after another
tumbling me out of bed early.

I watch you
just being you
because you can't not.

Me, doing this human gig?
It can be easy to not be me
until it's not,
and that is good.

This bolt you just tossed,
sharper, pointed,
landed right outside my window.
Still, I sit still,
humbled to witness you being fully you
while I be fully me
and take note,
"Be like lightning.
Don't be the lightning,
just be me."

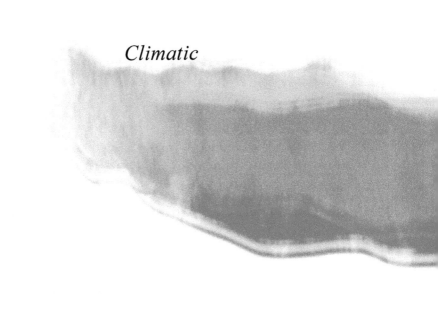

Climatic

I Am an Animal

Sometimes I forget I'm an animal
tamed too often by a manmade world,
Confined by constructs created in minds
that forgot who we are.

Egos handed hammers and nails
can only build big
then bigger
then biggest
until huge
becomes humorous to my humerus
and she just wants to leave.

I used to think my desire to flee was wrong,
still I fantasized.

How could I leave with the
goodness of life sitting on my shoulder?
My runaway would carry buckets of guilt,
a familiar flock of should monsters
demanding me to reason their way,
shaming me into the corner of
"who the hell do I think I am?"

I know.
I know who I am,
what I am
and it is not this thing
I watch play out
on screens made to suck us in.

Our earth's fury heats up.
Our son watches as western states burn
and says "thanks, guys"
knowing his inheritance
is a life on a suffering planet
divided by clashing beliefs.

People argue as if
the mean thing they say is true,
because so many mean things keep getting said
until mean merges with other meaningless unbelievables
that grow into new norms.

We shake our heads,
turn our heads,
and ignore this insanity
over and over again
sometimes for the sake of our own sanity.

Young Simba, heir in Disney's Lion King,
was fed a feast of fool's folly by evil
and believed he'd done the worst thing.
He hadn't.
Driven away,
so hard he tried to be who he wasn't.
Until in a dream,
he heard his father, Mufasa, say,
"Simba, remember who you are."
The hearts of the world he'd left
now lived in a parched land.
Scorched by the breath of ego.
Once dishonor displaced honor,
they were left without hope.

It was really not away
that I want to run.

It was toward
the truth of my tale.

I'd been tamed by
too many words,
outside wisdom,
should've and shouldn'ts,
would'ves and wouldn'ts,
Until I was spun into fool's gold
believing this is it.

Like Simba,
there was that moment
when what haunted was silenced.

No longer stalked
by voices not my own,
I remember
I am an animal
and rediscover that
inside the wilds of my being
is a truth that sets me free
and
a keen intuition eager to show me
the way forward.

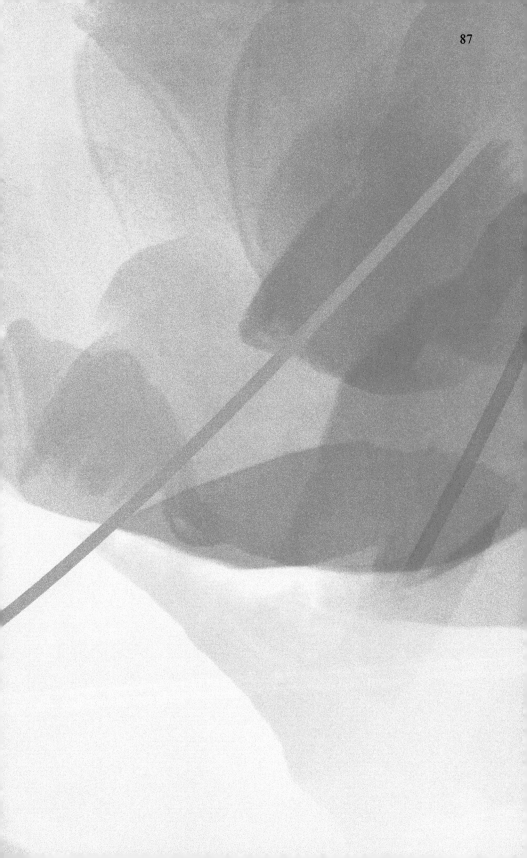

Earth Cries Out To Us

Sun reflects herself
off glass buildings
she knows not by name.
I cannot see her face
as she rises.
I cannot look upon her
steady path's fiery brightness.
I cannot ditch my awe
and forget the truth she brings.

Last Saturday night,
lying on a cushy couch,
I looked out the window
and saw Venus,
a star by her side.
I watched as they
moved with earth's rotation.

This big lumbering planet,
seared in civil unrest,
intensely divided,
as the warming of our globe
melts the polar bear's playground.
Earth cries out to us.
2,000 lightening bolts
strike fire and fear.

It doesn't have to be this way.

Dismissed warnings,
long ago predictions,
we barreled forward.

Chasing desire?
Boundless arrogance?
Bottomless belief that this land is ours?
Truth is-
we are vulnerable here
rotating around this sun.

Today I woke early
in another city,
Blinds opened,
Venus again
looks back at me.

Venus, I see you
and sense how small I am,
how small we all are,
and imagine our universe.
From how far away
can you and your star
see our land burning,
our seas churning?

Our planet's pain
cries out to us to stop
yet humans tweet more than birds now,
sunrises are blocked by erected buildings
as our seas choke on plastic.
While on our couches,
our soap boxes,
the universe reminds us how temporary we are,
but how long lasting our choices will be.

A Reflection of Descension

Reflections. Descensions.
Where are we headed?
A reflection of descension descends into places
familiar and unknown,
spirals forward and back until darkness laughs and says,
"Decide."

Unicycles without direction pace back and forth for balance,
Pacing pavement, searching hot on a globe too warm.

This thing you rest on, this thing you walk on,
this place between ozone and earth is alive.
Your source for breath,
Your source for nourishment,
Your source for gravity to keep your untethered self
from floating away.

Stop a minute, please.
Come sit here upon this hill with me.
Look beyond the limits of belief and eyes,
beyond a sense of knowing and declaration.

Still your breath until
you feel it slide in through your lips,
glide over your tongue,
and softly spill down through your throat,
extending your life.

Let your hands touch the soil beneath you.
Rest your palms flat until gravity holds you tight
and earth knows you know she's here.

Look up at the sky painted new for today.
Let it show you its story of moving forward,
recreating itself again and again.

Let your body rest on this earth that holds you.
Sense your senses remembering to wake up.

Let your ownership become relationship.

Let the heat of our earth
come only from the sun,
come only from the core,
come only from the passion of you being here now
responsible for caring for this place we call home.

For the Love of the Fox, the Himalayas, and the Jellyfish

Look at your feet.

You are standing
in black holes
of stale resistance.

Foxes go to war,
leaving their hunting,
shaking their heads,
knowing,

you cannot see,
what you
will not see.

"Sinking, I tell you, we're sinking"

Icebergs shutter at the stupidity
to not just sound the alarm.

Our Himalayas,
breathing
for the first time
since
manmade
remade
our earth.

Sleeping outside without cover,
my eyes fixed between familiar stars,

dots connect
channeling
facts from fictions
without resisting.

Addiction to right,
with nothing left,
invited jellyfish
to swim again
in clear Venetian canals.

We'll all swim along like this
until like bees swinging from trapeze,
we'll fall to our knees and pray to something.

Whatever,
whoever,
might still be willing
to listen to this cacophony of
"Help us",
Rising from hot currents
bubbling up through the contagion of delusions.

Part Two: Life

Emerge

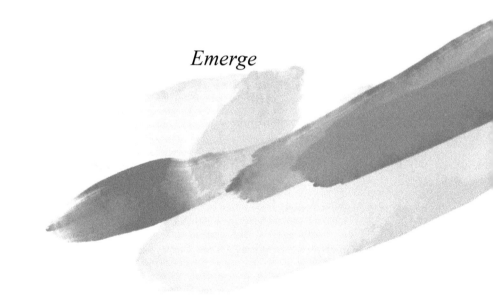

Like Cultured Cream

Like cultured cream,
becoming something I wasn't
made me forget my original ingredients.

An added teaspoon of this,
a bucket piled on top of that,
and voila.
There was not me.

A dollop of doubt,
a smidgen of smut,
until shaded windows
covered my eyes.

My light dimmed.

I faded.

For enough days now
I've wanted to walk away.
Not a dramatic exit.
just loosen what I hold tight,
allow it to flow to the floor,
and step forward.

One time I stood with my Mother
at the corner of 34th and 5th in New York City.

The elastic in her slip broke.
She giggled.

She felt it
let go of her waist,
slide over her hips,
barely brush by her legs,
suddenly puddling at her ankles.

When the light changed,
she walked forward
leaving that worn out covering behind.

Yesterday Drips Off My Belly

Inhaling,
breath expands my heart
awakens arteries of highways
leading to anywhere.

Rising,
Yesterday drips off my belly
as Today leaps up,
stares into my opened eyes.

Seeing,
she leans in resting nose to nose.
Relaxed, I giggle,
exhale, and sigh.

Remembering
I am home.
The therapy of her aroma
tickles trails opened
wide to possibility.

Stirring,
my senses sizzle to surface,
ignite together,
and today begins.

Playing,
we feel the music moving through my mind,
taste the crispness of morning air,
take a first step more alive into what will
tomorrow become yesterday.

Freeing,
what's to lose?
Unless I choose
not to move my piece
in the game of life.

In the Beyond of Knowing

My soul knows a knowing
my humanness
will never know.

In the beyond of knowing,
matter doesn't matter.

There I hear music
and crawl inside each note,
riding a wave of sound
that guides, revives, and whispers,
"This is who you are."

In the beyond of knowing
I sense bee and butterfly
calling me outside to play.
I go and learn how to pick the right flower
and bury my face deep into fresh delight.

In the beyond of knowing
I deeply breathe in new air.
It spills inside me.
I follow it in.
Together we sit in my untamed inner wilderness.
Ever more curious I ask,
"What do I most need to know?"

In stillness I wait
until new knowing
from beyond knowing
whispers guidance
for my next right step.

Let It Run

I am not old.
I am eternal.

Earth moans and sighs
as we pile upon her back,
hold on for life.

For life?
But what is life?
A birth and a death with days used up in between?
Moments that beat all before to be trumped by others
and then forgotten?
Breaths taken away, deepened, shortened, puffed?
Love met, requited, longed for, embraced?
Hope dashed, churned, adjourned, surmounted?
Dreams longed for, conjured, believed, achieved?

Perhaps.

Life is many.
Life is much.
Life is such and stuff with creme inside.
It rolls.
It crawls.
It walks and runs and climbs and falls.
It grows hair and pimples,
muscles and moods.
It is all we live for and what we fight to save.
It is rules and rhythms and sadness and joy
though it rips your heart out again and again.

It is finite.
I am not.

Loosen the reins.
Let it run.
It needs to be set free
until it is done
and returns to its roots to rest.

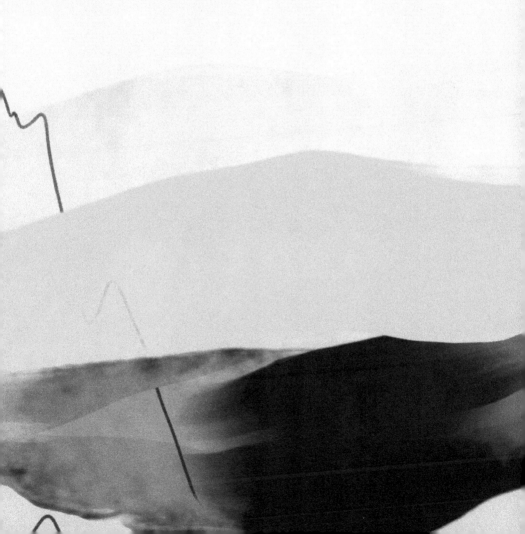

The Roaring Wave

When you discover who you really are
do not be afraid.
The world around you will do that for you.

When you discover in a moment that you are not peace
but instead the roaring wave lapping at the shoreline,
defining its next moment, go there.

Go there and celebrate
for the wild dance you declined
waited for you to stand up,
emerge, and raise your big voice.

When you discover
you cannot,
will not sell out again,
close the lid on the game.
Look them in their poker faces,
read what is real,
and quickly step away.

When you discover parts of you,
you might have never met,
curiously knocking at your doors and windows
begging you to let them in,
fling it all open!
Drop your chains,
leap into the expanse,
deeply breathe into your pure essence
perhaps for the first time.

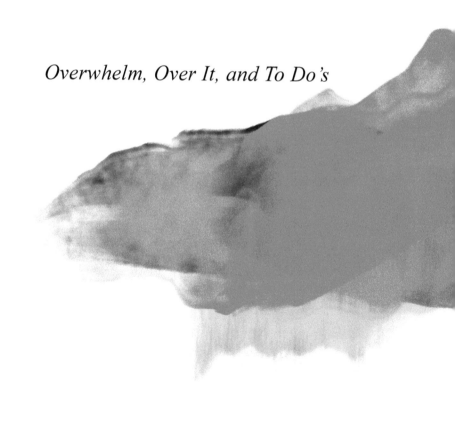

Overwhelm, Over It, and To Do's

Why Do I Have to Be So Good?

Why do I have to be so good?
In a world of cross your t's and dot your i's,
I'm a rebel who once sold out her being

Rules ruled our roost
until the chickens fled
one after another.
Not me.
I stayed and played out my role
longing to be loved.

Winds blew, houses fell.
Knights in duct taped armor
rode in on painted white horses
making the whole sappy soap opera
glisten with woe and
capture the poor ears of many.

Why not walk away,
remove the halo,
put down the shield,
and finally say, No?
No thank you. No more.
Not today or tomorrow.

Yesterday, my soul
slipped me a glance of her truth,
a taste of her sweet longings.
Today I cry on the front row of the
"Show Up and Be the Good Girl Life."

Soon before she who birthed me died,
her admonitions flowed for her soul knew
her being human would soon be done.
She spoke prophecy that quickly became truth.
Warnings that wander by my side
and cutely join me on the front row -
neatly dressed,
hair coiffed,
sitting up straight,
hands clasped tightly in their lap
until they hurt and bleed.

A wise one across the aisle says,
"Why are you here?
Your soul called.
She asked you out to play,
while you continue to worship
on the front row of the mother church
that died long ago.
She'd even said, 'Say no'.
Listen. Question.
Look around. Look within
and see all your soul shows you."

The way to walk away is to take just one step.
That next right step and then another
until fields open and mountains rise.
As your arms lift toward majestic skies,
gathered cloud's shadows dance around your feet
as you remember this is what you've longed for
the whole time.

The Love List

On a list of who I love where do I rank me?
On it? Off it? Top-five? Bottom five?
Forgotten to include me at all?

Each day do I listen to my wishes and dreams?
Does this life of service with an attitude of gratitude,
abstain from platitude, and stand up for both you and me?

Untamed fox,
I see you cross the Colorado road,
stop our car, stare at me as if to say,
"Remember the joy you feel in the wilds of your heart
when not attached to life's lists, the do's, and the don'ts.
For those are not you.

You, my sweet,
are the pig clock with wings
as it ticks off one second at a time
and smiles at the absurdity of absurdities.

You, my love,
are the one that once freed yourself
to crawl like a fox on your hands
and knees atop a French mountain
stalking the best view of morning's sky.
You found it looking up through grass blade's dew drops
as the juice of foreign berries
eaten right off the earth
dripped from your ruby stained lips.

You, my friend,
are the heart that seeks gracious love,

deeper connection, expansive compassion,
and the radiance that emanates from true self.

You, my playmate,
are the curious soul
longing for adventures in the depths of your being.
Delighting in the tiniest of things
as patterns reveal the truths of all we cannot see.
Tenaciously tickling the fancies of possibility
where stuck places give way to the all of what can be.

You, dear one, are love.
as you tether tight
from day to night
to Spirit where love flows more freely.

The fox has crossed your road,
stopped you with her tracks.
Her delight wakes you up even more to life.

See her there now at the foot of the mountain,
wild flowers in her face.
Quicken your pace, follow her trail,
and trust what happens next.

Mary Oliver Said

"Pay attention, this is your life!"
Yeah, yeah. aren't you just the wisest bearer
of brilliant news.

"Live your best life!"
Darn was I aiming for the worst?

These pie in the sky words
drip of privilege,
smell of other than.

Yet even when my longings are clear.
The mind comes along with rules and why nots.

Well, I'm tired of being good.
Mary Oliver said I don't have to be
so I'm done.
Done with holding back because someone said to.
Done with pussyfooting.
I'll clomp along like a dinosaur when that feels right.
I won't be one of those flip the switches from
good to bad.
I'll just be me.

Last night I dreamed I stood up to insanity,
but insanity believed in itself more than I did
so I just walked away.

The next room in my dream?
More insanity.
Women dismayed by what was happening.

I looked at them.
They looked to me.
All I knew was that I was hot
too many layers on me.
My feet shoeless, but wrapped in wool.
One by one I removed the layers
let them fall to the ground
and walked away.

I now paid attention
all I'd once paid distraction.

Am I stepping into my best life?
I don't know,
this whole gig is fleeting,
I'm just going to set my life free.

Me - Do = Be

From within this still place
there's nothing that needs to be done.

Nowhere to go.
Nothing to say.

Just breadth and depth.
Possibility and call.

Wild winds wane.
Wavy waters rest.

Me minus do equals be.

Just that.
Just this.

Seas Tossed Like Salad

Seas tossed like salad,
My inner tomato feels too ripe.

Words nonsensical and sensical
scramble to form shape
out of this roundabout time.

I remember little village England 1988.
Wrong side of the road driving.
Directions to exit,
but we couldn't tell where.
Round and round we went
'til confusion rose between us
and we laughed.

Where's laughter now
that laugh or cry
becomes ride or die
until I'm just tired.

You asked me what it'd look like
to add more alone time to my life.

I don't know.
I imagine expansive
wide open space.
Me at the edge
looking, pondering
before wandering
or maybe it'd just be
another exit-less roundabout.

Uninvited to do lists.
Thoughts seeded by others
and limiting ones watered by my
weary mind.
Feelings that churn just in case.
Fears and worries
round and round they go
blocking sweet truths I'd love to know.

More alone?
I'd ask my heart what she wants to do today.
Then I'd wait until she went round and round
as long as she wanted
knowing she's always already known the way.

The Razor's Edge

Out
of balance.
Too much
and
not enough
no longer
balance
each
other
out.

The continuum of so far left
and too far right
resists the middle
as it says
"This we've outgrown."

I know
I see
I feel
Yet time becomes a rhythm
whose beat I just won't feel.
And that's ok.

Owned by clocks
Washed up dry on rocks
My soul says no to this
go
go
go.

Out of balance?
 But of course!

Scales weighed by human time
remain precarious.

Teetering
on that razor fine edge
of more or less
I wonder how I got cut
while portals of possibility
open wide then close
unnoticed and abandoned.

Pay attention
A rich lesson is offered
for you who long to know.

No Matter What, I've Got You

Hello child, I've missed you.
Why wander the world of words
when time in our wilderness
brings you back home to me and to you?

One cannot be grounded
with roots ragged and frayed.

One cannot be grounded
with roots tucked shallow into infertile soil.

When wind blows you will fall,
when mind freaks you will listen
as my guiding voice becomes a distant memory.

First, stand up.
Feel the feet I made for you.
Spread them firm and wide under your beauty.

Now wiggle side to side,
up and down
until you settle
into the width
and breadth
of the you,
you reside in.

Feel the earth rise to meet you
and welcome you home again.

Breathe in me.
Exhale all else.

Breathe in fresh air
as the warmth of all that is
ancient and filled with love
rises up to mingle with the all of you.

Spirit reawakens and says,
I missed you. Welcome home.

The roots of your soul
reach deeply
through your feet.
You sway-dance
from side to side.

Storms blow through
as my wind whispers
softly in your ear,
No matter what,
I've got you.

Anchored, you remember,
the wilderness of your heart
and know without a doubt
it is there that I'm always waiting for you,
my dear beloved child.

Oh to Be List Less

Oh to be list less.
No have to's.
No need to's.
No nothing hovering
monstering me with should's.

To awake on the equinox
and stretch in bed.
Having wintered too long,
my muscles tight from hibernation,
too short to leap into spring.

I've become the bear in me.
My wildness briefly forgotten,
still lost in blueberry dreams.
I lift my paws high,
spread the pads of my feet,
notice the growth of my claws and laugh.
I drop them back to the bed.
Stretch into the length of me
as far as my reach
and the tip of my toes can go.
I'm delighted.

On this day,
When light and darkness are equal,
I lift myself gently from this wintering,
slip my feet onto the still chilly wood floor
and know I've survived.

To awake on the equinox without distraction
without voices waiting
without notes stuck to my desk
to do this or that,
I sigh with utter joy.

That last fall. That last winter.
They exhausted me.

Today, inside my heart and beyond my shutters,
red buds arrest my soul with pleasure,
painted yellow daffodils give way to lip red tulips,
dogwoods bark their delight,
cherry trees show me their inner blossom's freckles,
plump robins feast on fat worms,
nests busied, the Divine abounds.
Without hesitation,
I trade the to do's for tada's
and never return again.

Stuck to Unstuck

I Wake You Early

I woke early,
my heartbeat
pounding in my ear,
as if to say,
"Can you hear me?"

Are you listening
to the rhythm
I pulse through your veins
to ignite your soul
and fire up your spirit?

Can you hear the
difference in the symphony
minus one key chair
without your beat in it?

Can you feel the nuances of you
flutter in and out
with each breath feeding you hope?
Each exhale letting go of what
no longer fuels your soul?

Rolling on along as is,
you toss out flat sounds like
"I'm OK" and "All is Fine"
never reaching deeper to ask
"How are you, my heart?"

So I beat louder,
rise up into your ear
with primal sounds
to call you back to me.

Back to the wild woods of your soul
where growth is as simple
as a fallen acorn instinctively knowing
what is next.

I wake you early
to stir your being
and mix you up
until you rise
and wonder why.

Come now and sit with me on sacred land
until head chatter stops
and the woods whisper tales of who you are
and who they are
and how we all are
    whole,
        beloved,
            as one.

I wake you early
and pound my drums
to call you out,
set free your days,
loosen your breath,
and dance with you in wild earth's meadow.

Come take your place
beside the fox
below the hawk
upon what grows beneath
until you remember
you are so much more than fine
made tenderly whole again and again by the Divine.

Singleness of Heart

Heart divided,
   I strive to do better,
but my heart beats
   out of sync.

Heart divided,
   its strings pulled tight.
   tangled, confused
   by its longing,
   and questions of belonging.

Heart divided,
   I pause, I ponder.
   Feelings percolate
   as clarity bubbles up.

Divided hearts are mind made.
Hearts are soul made,
Whole, full, beating to a rhythm
distinct to the wild, raw sound of me.
Alive only through
the willingness to rise
and fall again and again.

A heart divided is
unheard
unknown
unreflective of the soul
it powers within.

That's all.

Pay attention not to the divide,
but to its sacred singleness.

Focus on what is true,
though it's messy

Focus on its circuits
though some aren't fully lit.

Focus on the good.
Follow the path in past the divide.

For in that depth – in the wilderness of my truths
the wholeness speaks
of the singleness that shines brighter
than spring sun behind clouds on rainy days.

Divvied Out

My mind wanders
    unsure of where to go
        with no direction from me.

Scattered and smothered
    like Waffle House hash browns,
she looks at me,
    arms thrown in the air,
        saying what do you want?

Divvied out
    a little here, a lot there
    until she snaps
    and digs her tired heels in deep

"Deep."
That's what she said.
"Deeper than you can see."

"What are we doing
    in this pile of life
        that's not ours?
            I just can't 'you' any more."

So she sat on the curb at the corner of
"I Don't Know How We Got Here" and "Done".

She then said,
   "Know your no's.
   Yes your yeses.
   In between is not your lane.
   So I'm not moving
   until you sit
   reboot our mind,
   reconnect with your soul,
   and remember which way is our way from here."

Stuck at the Crossroads

Stuck at the crossroads,
I spin my wheels and work extra hard to make
sure my emergency break is still on tight.
Engines revving while drive is firmly in park
makes me feel rebellious and up to something.

Stuck at the crossroads,
I split hairs about how I got here and
roll the dice on if I will ever leave.
Rutted paths leave no room for variance.
Earlier pilgrim's footprints fill with water
reflecting my aging dreams back at me.

Stuck at the crossroads,
the silver platters that held my dreams
are now tarnished and overtaken by kudzu.

Stuck at the crossroads,
I shudder at some of the choices that
propelled me through life.
The ones that flowed through heavy days
and realities I keep at bay.

Stuck at the crossroads,
I see I could be free.
I have the key and the chain is not even locked.

Stuck at the crossroads,
I grow impatient and take off my shoes.
I need to feel the dirt between my toes
and stretch them wide.
I need to scream
and remember when I quit dancing.

Stuck at the crossroads,
I consider my options and move slowly.
My body's compass pulls me toward the way
that would take me home by another road,
unfamiliar,
scary,
certain it is time.

No Words Need You Now Mutter

Spirit wanes.
I ask her where she's gone.

No answer.

Sigh.

So I leave her alone
and softly sing a lullaby.

Rest dear one.
May angel wings
wrap you tight.

Sleep dear one
until stars
reveal their light.

For you have churned
and turned so much milk to butter,

Feast upon the fat,
relax yourself,
no words need you now mutter.

A day can be whatever it is,
fluffy, flat, or scattered.

Just let it roll,
surrendered to
only that which matters.

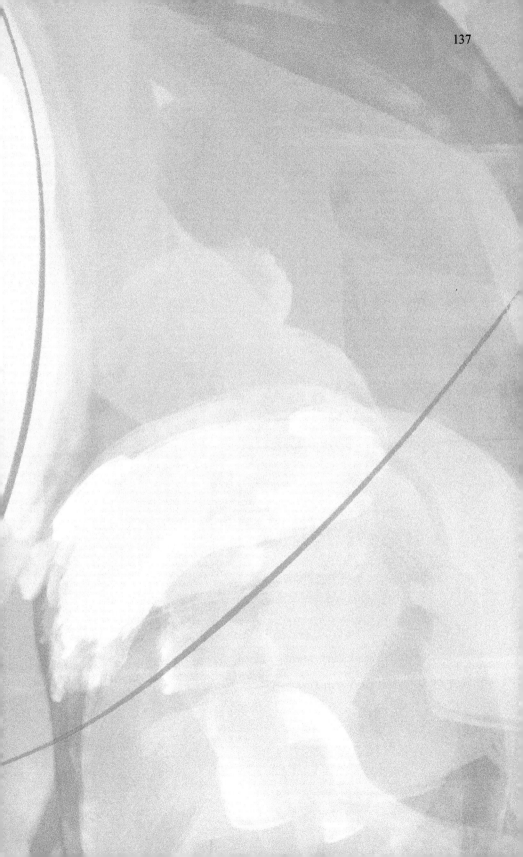

Rhythm Paced

Morning bird's song,
   verses perfectly paced,
   eight seconds silent,
   three seconds sung,

Rhythm,
   the thing
   I think I lost,

Morning bikers,
   her first, him behind
   lights on,
   arrive.
   Rhythm paced
   they turn.

I've been looking back
   where choices made
   once faded
   return to light
   to ponder.

I've been looking forward
   where unsure
   stalls today's known.

What to make of this?
What to make of this?

These things put before me
   until "Now" becomes
   a swirl of wondering.

Wonder.
   To be in wonder
   Without answers.
   To be in process
   And just notice.

Morning bird knows
   the song of "Now".
Her there on the limb
   outside my window,
She who sings
   the rhythm for this day,
Awakens my day
   to soul's simplicity,
Guiding me so much deeper
    than the tangle of threads
    in my mind.

Now.
Here.
That's all there is,
Anyway.

My Mind, She Sighs

My mind, she sighs.
Pushed for too long now.
Overridden like a saggy-back horse.
Under appreciated.
Set on a path too long.

Exhausted.

Too much has been asked of her.

Today now simplified to rectify,
I climb off my high horse,
help my mind down from her worn horse,
take her hand,
and walk towards a meadow
where nothing
more than awe
is asked of us.

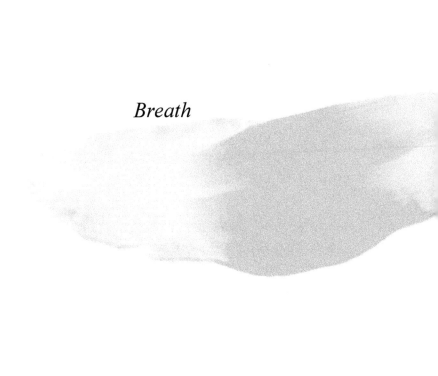

Breath

We All Got Something

There's hope in these breaths,
playfulness in these thighs,
yet I hold my breath
to see what the state around me will be.
Sometimes hostage to truths I don't want to see.

We each "got" something –
Something real,
Something tight,
Something to weave into noose that can
stop our breath with fear.

We all got something that races our heart
through closed fields with little room to move.

We all got something that we don't want.
Something we'd trade in at the lost and found
for anything better than this thing.

Why'd we not get only good
so we could be good and do good
for the good of all that's good?

Why'd we not get the fairytale life
where knights shined their armor bright enough
to cast light on all darkness,
where Cinderella's midnight never struck,
where Goldilocks got everything she wanted
without the danger of bears?

Because
there's nothing
rich enough or deep enough
handed out on silver platters
to open our eyes to what is real in our souls.

What is alive behind the eagerness of my eyes
longing to show me the way?

What I got is at the crossroads of spirit's will and mine.
It's where we meet through my surrender to learn
who and why I am.

What I got to deal with, work with,
learn to navigate through is my depth,
the richness of the lessons they teach me
about love, compassion, and hope.

Can't give back what I got –
malady, challenge, or foe.
I can take it in my arms,
love it because I can't leave it,
embrace it because it holds the clues
to all that is divinely rich in purpose and possibility.

It's what I got and it's got me.

Trust the Breath

My breath is caught this morning,
not taken away.
Caught between a hook and a rung,
not deep,
not shallow.

My breath,
she's just sitting in my chest,
like stilled wind on a too hot summer day,
like a smooth surface pond.

On this day she just doesn't make sense
to the sensible.

Still winds and smooth ponds
subtly move at the surface,
while underneath - life goes on.

Breath caught.
Held taut.
Suspended between this moment
and anticipation of another one coming.

I watch her
and surrender to this liminal space
between
this and that -
that moment where trapeze artists
let go of the fly bar,
and suspend in air
before the catch bar arrives.

I cannot grab what's not yet here.
I cannot grab it if I hold on to what was.
I cannot grab it if I hold on to what is.
I cannot grab it unless at this time I let go, leap,
and trust.

My breath here -
stilled by choice
needs this moment,
this in-between the bars moment,
to look back at what was
and forward into what is to come.

I trust her.

My breath and I know liminal -
We know how to let what we've loved
end as we knew it.
We know how to pause,
reach open handed
and trust that what comes
will take this life
to a next that arrives
at the right next moment.

That time will come.

On this morning
I sit and breathe softly -
with my breath caught so perfectly
held lovingly by my heart.

Notice

Newspaper man arrives with yesterday's news.
Talking heads wake,
prepare to pontificate on one tired subject.

Sky, didn't look right
too bright,
too blue for 4:30am.
Now she rinses off our dust,
shakes us up to say I am here and so are you.

So breathe.
Deeper.
No, much deeper than that,
until it pours through to the floor of you,
stirs your roots awake,
anchors you through random storms
that brighten dark skies
way too early for sleeping minds.

Breathe and ponder this later.

A single strand of rain drops catches my eye.
Street lights spotlight the fresh fallen bounty
from clouds too full to hold tight any longer.

One drop then another,
separated by wind and gravity,
sparkle in the light
drip quickly to touch earth below
but not for the first time.

Evaporation,
condensation,
precipitation,
the water cycle unresisted
comes around again to say,
Notice.

Me, you – it's the same –
surrender to the rise,
nestle in the clouds
until you're released,
sparkle on the way down,
soak into where you land,
briefly shine in new light.

The Fullness of Me

I sigh
to catch my breath.
Her, so shallow, so fast.

Set free she turns to look
back at me panting.

"My breath" I say
"What do you need?"

She says,
"Your presence, your awareness
space to move in the
way I was made to move.
Slow then full then deep into the core of you.
Your lungs ache to expand
into the fullness of me.

I am your breath
yet you cap me off at shallow
and wonder why your head spins dizzy
and life feels suddenly off kilter.

I, that first gasp you took
when I met you at birth
to bring you to life.
Without me,
you would die.

We live in a time where
fear of losing breath
has shallowed that which is meant
to pour into your body.
As your senses sense the texture,
the temperature of me,
you ask Divine to speak and I come.

Breath of life.
This dis-ease-
this virus can take breath away,
but don't most people do so daily?

Stop and let me fill you.
Let me slow you down
until your awareness expands,
welcomes the fullness of me,
and you remember
what it's like to breathe deeply again."

Scream

Waves come fast.
Prepared, I grasp hold of what I can
knowing I can't control the ocean.

Drowning was my specialty.
Strapping my ankle
to heavy bottom coral
while asking for help
was my pattern woven by habits.

They choked the breath out of my lifetime.

Timelines carved onto paths
that twist and curve
confuse everyone
so my truth can't be followed.

Held breath
builds strength for lungs
that will someday scream,
"Stop"
at me who strolls along
as if all is okay.

My parts,
the ones who live inside of me,
sit this morning in the shadows
unwilling to play
this game of hide,
but don't be seeked.

Weary, I untie my ankle from the coral.
Effortlessly, I float to the surface.

Last flickers from dark sky's stars,
ease my welcoming back to breath.

Buoyed by the fat of salvation
I need not swim.

Relieved,
my lungs inhale
all that is fresh
pulling in deep
the calm of the night.

Abruptly their longing
to let go, did.

Guttural screams ensued,
as the heavens reached down their mighty hands
to stir sound into a symphony of belonging.

"Scream," they said,
"For your heart aches,
your being quakes,
real life shakes worn out roots.

Old anchors tied to heavy coral cut, bind.
They held tight
when life's fight was human made,
but you are not.

Floating on this surface
as moon begins to pack it in for the night,
scream, sigh, slap the water
until you begin to remember who you are.

Already whole.
Complete.
Made in an image
that only needs to be reflected
on your path forward.

The others,
the ones you love,
the ones you ache for,
must be set free to float
under early morning moon,
and feel the touch
of last minute stars
twinkling on their face.

For this is life.

Release roots formed from fear and control.
Trees cannot grow from sources disconnected
from reality.

For now, float here
until morning sun stretches her first ray
warmly caressing your cheek,
awakening what went dormant within.

Hear the song of the seas
echoing back your screams
to let you know
you are alive,
held,
and loved.

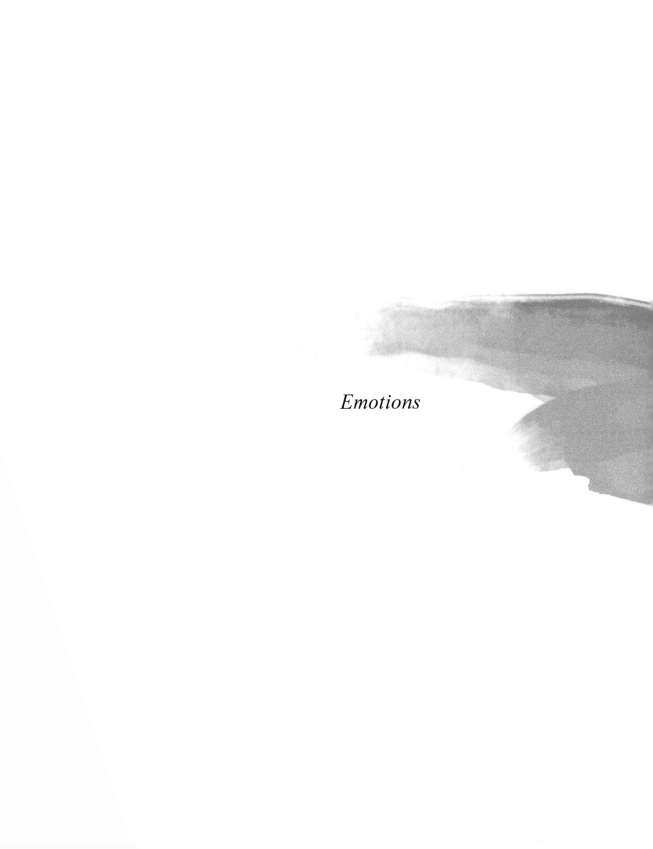

Emotions

Fear Knot

Fear knot.
Tangled in emotions,
tripping over my self,
Stumbling. Stopped. Seeing.

This business of being human,
feeling the feels
way, too, big.

Trapped, too tight
for breath squeezed dry
before swallowing.

Connected through disconnecting,
forced to stop quickly,
rear ended by reality
waking up in the wilds.

What do we do
when the tiger's
this close?

Breathe,
count to 10,
turn,
look him in the eye
and remember
who you were
before
the world tamed you.

Fear not.

But Still I Love

Mourning dove sings out a single rhythm of verse,
sits in silence 'til I think she won't sing another one.

Reminds me of my dying mother,
the long empty space
between her last breaths
until there wasn't another.

Untying too tight mama heartstrings
leaves me wobbly wondering what's next.

Small plane flies low
Can't see it. Just know it's there.

Front window shakes.
Hanging glass heart rattles,
clings a ting against the glass it hangs upon.

I've hung my heart like fine Victorian drapes
on walls too big for it to cover.

I've hung my heart on dreams unfolding
before I heeded their small print warnings.

I've hung my heart on unmended fences
that fell with wind's slightest touch.

But still I love.

Even bigger now,

Through friction before anything
beautiful comes from it,

Beyond last breaths
until my own breath deepens again,

Within untying strings
weighing down new wings for flight,

Within things that can be seen even if I can't
understand them.

Some Days Feel too Tight

Washed clean again and again,
nature's baptism shines through my windows.
Candlelight fills my room.

Some days feel too tight,
just not right before they even get a chance
to breathe their longings into this space.

Four days ago
doubt and despair
cozied up with my heart.
Shallowing my breath,
casting a spell,
tangling hope and miracles
in kudzu vines creeping closer.

How can I know tomorrow
or the flowers of spring
when I'm sitting in the dark
stillness of an inner winter?

Who am I to worry about
things that take my breath away
before the air of their being
has even gasped a newborn's first breath?

5 doors down the bright blue bug light
swings in the wind on that upstairs porch
beckoning little beasties into its snare.

The owner who hung it
was found dead last Thursday,
unaware of today's rain
and things to worry about come spring.
Stories say a cloud of sadness wrapped
itself around that house and swallowed that man whole.
Addiction gulped up his hope
and flushed his future down drug's drain.
Numbed now, the only
light shining at that little shotgun home
daunts, dares to snare more death.

Rain quiets.
My eyes shift focus to seven candles surrounding me.
Lit early they bring some peace to this tangled day.

Breath deepens enough to reach in
and release doubt and despair
from the snares of my shadow self.

My soul pulls breath even deeper
expanding my gut
so inspiration can stir my senses,
stretch my being beyond this space
that feels so small.

Waterfalls of Melancholy

Gathered tears hang over me in heavy clouds.

Capacity reached,
sanity breached,
waterfalls of melancholy
pour over my shoulders
smoothing my jagged edges.

Broken dams
reclaim denied spaces
as control gives up.

So I sit
and wait
until better does something
to improve today.

Dammed tears
smell of angst
from fought back struggles
amidst their longing
to just flow.

Nonsense –
my senses just can't make sense of this,
because they can't.

Fast flow happens when the dam breaks.
Grace steps in when we let it flow.
The rest will rest once it's freed
and teach me what I need to know.

The Un-dodge-able Demands of Despair, Disdain, and Dismay

Breath falls in short
lands hard.
Belly longs for air
caught between inhale
and hold.

Chest tight.
World around tight.
Energy stirs up trouble
between here and peace.

Words swirl into knots.
Despair, disdain, dismay,
feel their way forefront.

Seen, not yet heard,
They ride in on waves
un-dodge-able.
One by one they line up,
Demanding voice,
Holding deep breaths hostage
Until I've stopped.

They shake me awake.
"Listen, you are lost."

Way past the corner of bitter and sweet.
Long past the rest area of calm in chaos
Now past the knowing
that
this
is
not
where you're meant to be.

Anxiety arrives to say
not this.
Not this now.

She shakes your limbs,
stirs your roots,
saying move away from this.
This that holds your breath,
diverts your path,
steals your peace,
and hides your joy.

Go ahead and be shaken.
Drop the leaves you've
tied to your tree,
embellished as if they belong.

One breath,
shallow at first.

One long exhale.

Next breath a bit deeper.

Exhale longer.

Breath trapped slowly moves.

Shallow living's sighs
rise one after another.

As you hear,
"It's OK. You're OK."
Just sit here and breathe
'til dust settles
and precious next path
takes your hand
and leads you forward.

168

Press Pause

Floating
between this and that,
my fear's
afraid to land.

It's OK.
You're OK.
You and me, we are passing through
aspects of the soul.
We are here
doing a human gig
when human gigging
feels more like frog gigging.
Our dance with life
tainted by pitch forked words,
unhinged anger,
unhinging doors
not meant to be opened
like that.

So we float
between words unsettling
incited, recited, over and over again.

How does a soul passing through
not grab hold of all of this
and make it real?

What is real?
My scattered self reeled in
in this moment.
Early in this new day,
darkness still surrounds me
streetlight's steady watch
bare branches' crisp shadows
paint shadow pictures between me and daylight to come.

Imagine a view from above
this world. All of this
and press pause.
There I see tangles
webs woven from powerful words,
deep longings
stuffed angers
frictions mounting until
the tectonic plates within this rhetoric
rubbed, scraped, shifted, and broke.
Upset had upset the upset within.

What to do now?

Step back,
breathe deeply
power down mind chatter's cacophony
until breath settles with this moment
near my heart.
No longer floating
I find my center within.
Ancient
from a time before this,
will continue on beyond this.
More aware, responsible.
I own my part in the story
choose words wisely
listen and tend to my emotions
and take one next step forward.

Denied Tears

Fresh tears rise to the edge
and fall full of all I feel inside.
Joy, sadness, loss, lost.

One after another
they gather together
to express what words cannot.

Change has happened
but syllables are not enough
to wrap my un-knowing around my heart.

A day has come
I knew we'd walk to.
My heart feels its presence
and I begin to wonder about
all the tears I denied.

The ones that rose
and I yanked back down.

The ones I chose not to feel out of fear
or I was moving too fast.

The ones I felt fully
and swallowed until my soul began to choke.

Drowning in uncried tears,
I learned to swim pretending I was OK.

Stale saltiness
burned my eyes.

Ducts made for release
stung at their presence,
until last Monday,
when without resistance,
they flowed again.

Tears
because I will miss
what is
as it becomes what was.

Tears,
for kindness I cherished
and the gratitude they bring.

Tears,
for the fear of change
that must come for
new stars to align.

Tears
for tears never cried,
Tears denied and deemed unworthy,
unimportant, or not OK in that moment.

Uncried tears
had untethered me from you.

So I cried all day,
fell into their flow,
because I knew
they knew a truer path home.

Hope

Little bird's shadow
awakens my smile.
Strings of chirps follow.
Moment sung into being,
New day has begun.

This early hour,
when most still sleep,
light slowly parts the darkness
as I sit alone listening.

Candles flicker.
Glass reflects back
this early day's rhythm
that I love so much.

I've walked a disrupted path,
played havoc with my life.
Unsettled emotions over and over again
tossed my inner sea.

Seized by fear,
gripped by anxiety,
my eyes searched for the shoe
that would surely fall next.

I almost did me in,
one step away from done.
Each shallow breath,
barely brushed my lungs.

Some part of me
must have longed to live.
That voice, distorted by disruption,
lifted up one syllable,
"Help."

The greater than what loomed,
the hope of better to come,
the letting go of a past,
moved me forward,
led me to this softer morning
where shadows no longer startle,
stillness deepens my breath,
as new day begins.

Tethered Tight

Cradled at the foot of mountains,
they surround me,
they astound me,
and beckon my heart to venture beyond
boundaried thoughts.

Fear breeds fear
when faith is empty.

I know empty faith.

Full to the brim
with self-will,
I snuffed out
the light aching to shine within.

Dimmed,
I felt safer.
All the bright lights
I knew invited danger,
but lights meant to shine
don't dim easily.

The consequences of not
being bright sear the heart within.

Surrounded by these mountains,
I remember I am eternally held
by something bigger than fear.

The layers within these mountains
yield the majesty they bring.
The layers of my life add up to me.

My will, my worries, oh yeah, I can stray,
but held by something mighty,
tethered tight to something greater,
my light becomes just enough willing
to shine.

Listen

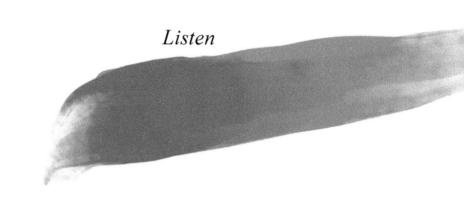

Biology of Being

Ache.
Core of my being
deep in my soul,
I weep.

Bumble Bee
bumps into my windows.
Furry Pup
growls like every day.

As our world stands still
waiting for wave after wave
of a rising tsunami.

All this we made
cannot stand up against
the biology of being.

Things happen.

Viruses spread
from the wild
to the tamed
without immunity.
Meanwhile we shelter in
and those who can
bravely step out into harm's way.

I remember curfews.
The day Rev. Dr. Martin Luther King Jr. was assassinated
a few miles from home.

My grandmother wept with fear
as my mom left to take care of the most vulnerable,
the children.

I was just a child, too.

Houses locked up tight.
Tensions rose
as military arrived to separate us
until our city
could breathe
together again.

Different. But the same.
Another bad thing has happened
and our world
must never
be the
same again.

Both came with warnings
but we pushed forward

Our world is begging for change.
It is time we remove our blinders
and listen.

Unrest

Hearts,
like
over
stretched
rubber
bands,
break.

I hear you
scream out
your pain
your fear
your rage.
Just
so much
unjust
justice.

Marching.
Quaking.
Tombs
full of
unknown
soldiers
shaken
open
wide.

Factions'
frictions
divided,
united
now
in
unrest.

Minds,
tangled threads
from centuries
of
better than,
less than.
Equations
that
will
never
add up
to
love.

Anger
boils
within
without
peace.
Hot lava
just can't
not
flow.

Babies' force fed
warped realities,
brimming
beyond
capacity,
spill
over.

Broken, cracked.
Broken, open.
Trapped screams
rise up big
rise up bold

through hands shaking
one word loose
from trees planted
in soiled soil,
"Stop!"

Life's been
shut in,
shut down.
Trapped,
too long now.
Pressure cooker days.
Dazed.
Ghost virus
hangs in droplets.
Civil unrest
hangs in news.
Either,
when
swallowed,
take
our breath
away.

Vicissitudes
vacillate
violently.
Pendulum
swings
between
extremes
until
its
fixed point
breaks
and
falls.

Balance,
not left of it,
not right of it
yearns to be found
outside our tangled mind.

Last night,
I watched a man
lead a march.
Passionate.
Peaceful.
"Hydrate," he said.
"Follow," he said.
"Chant," he said.
Gut ache,
ancient,
loosened
bellow out
what'd been stuffed
from
shallows shaping societal self,
cultures hierarchically made,
choking
essences'
from
being.

"Sit," he said.
Here on this hill
Where in front of you
another marching man's
civil rights got shot.
"Sit," he said.
Here on this hill
and listen
until

your voice,
the one down deep,
your truth,
the one you were born knowing,
stills,
breathes deeply,
rests.

Light
will find
its way
through
this darkness.

Resilient,
we will
rise
until
integrity,
whole again,
restores
peace.

And She Smiled Back

Pandemic mind wanders
like her namesake.

Information overload.
Do this. Do that.
Until she says,
"I just can't."

Yesterday,
she ate a big bowl of blueberries,
hoping their sweet
would tame
the tart of life.

She stared at talking heads,
read woven words,
as tales of life and death,
brought her day to a halt.

Still she barreled through
dragging
her mule of a mind forward
because
Sitting in the mud of her mind
felt indulgent.

The world clammers,
'Let's get on with it,"
as if we can ever be the same.

No longer a virgin pandemic mind,
she can't unsee,
she can't unknow.
What once was possibility
is now very real.

Those who know,
know horrors and truths
that shake
and
rattle foundations.

Those who doubt
haven't seen
what those who know
can't ever forget.

Like towers collapsing,
the air hasn't cleared enough
for senses
to make sense
of this.
This moment
so full of loss,
inviting profound change
or not.

Pandemic mind is new,
popped up on the screen,
a million questions,
few answers,
changing every day.

Candle light flickers
guiding her swirling mind from left to right
as words
pour themselves across her journal's page.

Early morning sky colors
wandering from dark to deep baby blues
peek in
nudging her more awake.

Eyes open wider.
She looks left,
sees Venus over her shoulder,
her mind hushes.

In this stillness she hears
a bigger voice within,
"Go see sun's rise."

And she does.

Pink skies welcome her to another window.
New day invites her to begin again.

As pink pulls orange forward
and
soft clouds bounce light between each other
a reflection emerges.

Words whisper to her softly,

"Though darkness might seem foreign
darkness is just darkness.
Planets still shine like stars.
Sun still rises behind clouds.
Go,
reflect light
be light
share light.
Help each other find their way."

Pandemic mind
sighed
and
softened.

The beautiful sunrise
smiled at her
and
she smiled back.

When Words Don't Come

When words don't come
I get lost in music.
Bold beats take me elsewhere.
Move me along,
past my stuck places,
sad faces,
where worry seems in a hurry
to take us on a journey to Nowhere.

Meanwhile,
Somewhere sits and waits for me.

Forward.
Move forward.
That's all I gotta do.

Meditation time bounced today
from Jesus' lesson of living water
to Tina Turner chanting with children.

Our world,
most days disconnected
now connected
by words rampant.

Widespread pandemic,
dis-ease of disease,
rattles our rafters,
sends us apart
and draws us together.

Life's laboratory,
its lessons and remembering,
successes and failures,
teach.

I wonder,
will we learn.

The Wilderness
~A dialogue with the Wilderness who today chose to call me Kitten~

Kitten,
why don't you play more?
Your joy is buried just under the surface,
always wanting to take your hand,
but you prefer to suffer.

I'm telling you that gig is up.
Joy is jumping too often
and
your "I can't"
or
"I'm too old"
or
"they didn't teach me",
sound like the wah, wah, wah,
of a toddler put to bed for the nap
he most needs
and will eventually succumb to anyway.

Kitten, tell me what you're tired of.
No don't.
You'll fondle those worn out tales
like musty old furs at a vintage shop.
Again your wah, wah, wah's.
– You know –
just put them down.

The past?
Let it be.
Go ahead and dig around
for treasures in its compost pile.
See what's growing that's sexy fresh and wildly raucous.
Bring that into your recipes for life.

I need you to help others
through their stuck place.
Their joy and other good stuff
might be hidden deep
so bore a hole of light with love
to help them breathe again.

The world is on a ventilator.
Shallow breaths cheat our hearts
from oxygen that fuels our soul
and moves us forward.

Wilderness, what more do you ask of me?"

Kitten,
turn to the light.
Feel the light.
Be the light.

Wilderness,
That's just too broad.
You don't know this human gig.
It's often insane out here right now.
Toxic, tangled,
up is down and down is up.
Hugs could be deadly,
quarantine fatigue set in,
now we reemerge wobbly.

Kitten,
go ahead and die to this thinking.
Die to playing small and fearing breath.
Fear not breathing,
fear holding your breath
because of fears meant to be let go.

Get your groove on.
Forget about goals.
Step into a better vibe,
let it shake you free.

You're just here to be you.
Nothing to compare you to.
Like Sister Carole said,
"Kitten you are unique. Everyone is."

If nothing else sticks from our romp –
remember I've got you.
Always.

Choices

Settle down.
Weary,
you can't row your boat
merrily down or
up the stream.

Wise sage said
don't push the river,
but you've scooped it
all up in your arms
and carry it on your back.
It's not yours to push or carry,
nor is the world.
Not like this.

Desperate measures
aren't adding up.

We're all in this river together.
Dammed we're divided.
Divided we fall and drown.

Tread.
Tread water
for the long haul
from here to there.
The pandemic's pandemonium
drowned out the sounds
of earth tipping its axis
to wake us up.

Birds still chirp.
Squirrels still forage.
Azaleas open as tulips bow and exit left.

This world's a stage
and this can be
our finest act.

If we stop.
and
trade arrogance for humility,
cash in criticism for praise,
swap cruelty for humanity,
ditch judgment for peace.
Choices,
many on the table.
What will we choose?

These Are the Wilds

What would happen if we all just stop?
Even when sent to our corners
we are still so busy.

Those who have to do, have to do.
Those who don't could pause, still the air
and not stir up so much in the wilds.

These are the wilds,
that place where pavement ends,
and roads wind to a close.

This is where the known ends
and innovation begins.
This is where route ceases routine
and winging it becomes progress.

What do moments made a mess teach us?
Where might we resist?
Here to listen.
Here to love.
Where to go from here?

On the Other Side of Knowing

Sun's rising earlier now.
Birds' unbroken song rhythm,
sets pace for this new day

The unknown of what was to come a year ago
now marks the last of what then was normal.
My friend, Sister Carole said,
"You've got one goal. Come out alive."
On this day I'm still here.
I pause to remember those who aren't.

If I knew then what I know now,
I'd have done the same things.

Before knowing,
there was curiosity.
Concern and worry tagged along.

Still there's something marked
about any profound before and after.

Today my vocabulary is expanded,
heartache more perfected,
longing stretched to limits.

Vulnerability wore herself out months ago,
no longer virgin to pandemic.

Now on the other side of knowing,
I'm even more thankful
morning bird's cadence
continues to pace me forward.

Part Three: Self-Portrait

Fish Out of Water

Fish out of water,
thirsty.
Shallow breaths never drop deep
enough
to awaken my soul.

I reside here,
    but I am not here.
Invisible,
    I do not fit in.

Addiction down,
powerless,
I reach for your hand
warm to touch.
Soul sighs.

She remembers and reminds me -

My younger feet walked
upon tree's raised roots,
balancing importance and confidence
upon deep-seated joy.

My younger eyes feasted
upon the world as playground
filled with roly-polys.

My younger hands carried
An imaginary kitten
And was never alone.

My younger heart swelled
with simple love
overflowing with silly laughter.

Time to step outside of me,
to look and see my construct
built for survival.
Storm shelters stocked with worry.
Memory deposits getting dull.
Fickle fortresses full of fight.

I reside here,
    but I am not here.
Invisible,
    I do not fit in.

My imagination wanders off with my soul self
to a new place where people play and love,
where creation is the delight of day
and a lone ladybug wandering
down the sidewalk on Main Street
is worth protecting from the feet
of those barreling forward.

I am here,
I am alive,
I am me,
so I let me be.

Breathing in I feel
the cool morning air spill through
pouring down my throat
like a waterfall dammed for too long.

Lungs expand to catch her bounty
as my ribs open wide
willing to welcome the all of this.

Breath pours through me
until torso twirls,
fingers tingle,
and toes wiggle with joy.
Breath of life stirs up all within me.

Me,
a soul having this human experience,
giggles with delight,
lets constructs go,
and returns to walking on roots
that tell true stories
I came here to remember.

Melting Into Wonder

Melting into wonder,
I spill over my edges.

Fluid buttery essence of my being
freed to play naturally.

Shaped by molds now cracked.
Oceans of memories swept away.
No longer the need to make sense.

Looking back
pulled me back
into arms that held too tight.

Molds broken,
eyes opened,
I see clearly again.

What I Did Wasn't So Bad

What I did wasn't so bad.
Leaving my kids
just for the night,
but I knew it was more
than that.

There was a poster.
Later a call.
Later a moment
when in front of the house I thought,
why not?
Because the hell I was in, was me.

Odd house, Victorian, colorful, not smooth,
Rough enough to shake me loose.
Self strangled, I gulped up a few words,
then a thousand poured.

Her, sitting on a skin,
tapping a little gong,
accent, somewhere on the floor, between here and there.
Her smile so wide it melted me.

Me and her theater in the round,
I sat,
dripping sweet,
rocking upon the little chair.

Yeah well that was then.
She poked my sweet, released other drippings
so I came back until
nowhere else felt like home.

On Tuesdays the now sanctuary smell of pesto and pasta
wafted the all of me
back under the spell.

(For Valentine and the Memphis Writer's Ensemble)

The Page

I've been avoiding you.
You once a piece of tree
all smooth and lined now.

There's something about the way
the movement of this favorite pen
spilling ink across your body
pulls the deepest me onto the surface
and into your light.

Lately, tangled mind snared my words,
hoarded their hope,
wound them too tight to talk.

I've danced around you air writing like 90's air guitar.
Poetic lines floated like an old typewriter's ribbon
loosed from its reel.
Real life too tight, your virgin space offered space
too vulnerable for this.

You, my mistressed affair,
too seductive and scary for me.
There's no room in the world
for the wild my inner animal longs to be.
There's no room in my mind
for me to just walk away.
Not because I'd leave you,
but because I long to find me.

See,
you slick, refined once a tree
I come here and the very touch of you
begins to set the lost touch within me free.

She, who you always knew,
has flirted with you for years,
waltzed into your arms,
lived for that last verse's dip,
and relished every world sealed with word's kiss.

Born to play upon your ground,
grounded by the grace of your space,
knowing you helps me know me,
reveals what you see,
        what you hear,
        what you sense.

I already know
or just don't want to today.

I trust you even now
when my trust feels most broken.

You,
like a snake charmer's sharp pungi sound,
slowly rising the cobra's head,
have me held within your trance.
My eyes glazed,
my body swaying,
until entranced,
my truths rise.
Freed ink now covers your surface
and I see clearly what felt like hell to keep inside.

My wild released,
she refuses to ever be tamed again.

Island of Surrender

I became an island of myself.

The gulf became an island between us.

The island in my kitchen must be clear
within that granite space to calm our home.

Islands.
Many.
Floating away.
Distanced from.
Not yet discovered.
My imagination secretly desires them all.

My world felt too small for so long.
I binged on the delights of both sweet and deadly
in hopes of expanding from within
what felt squished from without.

Still, today when the writer lady
prompts me to ponder an island
and write from there,
the part of me that's, metaphorically speaking,
a mermaid, leapt with joy.

The part of me still trapped is already there.
The part of me that longs incessantly
to explore has already arrived.
Still, words don't weave easily.
The vista of a space beyond this one
I've been confined to for so long doesn't easily emerge.

So I sit and wait.
I imagine the basics, palm trees,
tall, cold to the touch.
Branches too high to reach,
moved by winds too high to feel.
Present only to my sight.
There are the gratuitous coconuts
strung closely together.
My taste buds tingle at thoughts
of fresh cracked coconut milk
spilling from above.
My mouth opens wide to its nectar
overflowing beyond my lips,
dribbling down my cheeks,
my chest, the tan of my belly,
the heat of my thighs,
until there, right here in this writing, I arrive.
My island, the one my imagination conjures,
now spills like a spell across my skin.

Sun's rays reach closer without permission
though I willingly welcome the stroke of their fingers.
Willowy, sinewy, lacing their corseted magic around my soul.
Too relaxed to walk,
I slowly crawl to water's edge,
sand exfoliating my skin from prior day's drama

Shell chips stick to my sweaty body.
The sea's remains glitter against me as a wave arrives,
kisses my fingers, my toes, my eyes awake.

Why stop here?

On this island, my island,
I roll into the surf,
upon the surf,
positioning myself to surrender myself
to being propositioned in whatever form she arrives.

An island of surrender.
Yes, that's it,
it arrives with the next yes,
and the next yes,
until the nexus of these moments
carry me home more alive and in peace.

Miss Well Behaved

The quietest thing is now no longer quiet.
Squashed, her voice, that is,
Squished between truth and behaved
Suddenly it, her voice, screamed.

Her so very properly trained,
obedient like a well schooled pup,
contained like a correctly sealed and burped Tupperware bowl
became bitterly done like a 1970s over baked
upside down pineapple cake.

We watched.

There was something eerily stunning to witness
as those first sounds gurgled up
out of pipes long since flushed through.

Well really long since used.

Why in this moment must she no longer be the quietest?

Seriously, after all these years
of sculpting, crafting, defining
her character sketch so sweetly,
now,
with one screech after another bubbling up
we all ran for cover.

Once a month our TVs take over our viewing choice
to test their government alert system.
For those necessary but annoying minutes,
there's choice to listen or mute.

Here, bearing witness to her chasm's creation
we have no choice.

In this unexpected leap from "as we knew her to what is this"
just as we fear for our ears, she stops.

Ahhhhhhh, the beauty of her quiet again.

The relief that she's remembered who she was told to be.

The relief that soon, Miss Well Behaved, will behave.

We collected our sighs of relief,
tied a flowered ribbon to an old Easter basket,
put them inside and gifted them to her.

But she, her voice, laughed.
One by one she took our collection
and tossed them cliff-ward.
Yes, off the edge
and into the abyss as the echoes of our sighs
reverberated back up to her as yeses.

She grabbed their echoes,
all of them like helium filled balloons,
until lifting lightly, playfully,
she soared willingly, joyfully
towards whatever waited on the other side.

Her voice,
the one set free,
giggled and never looked back.

Your Body is an Animal

Your body is an animal.

Needs to
move,
stretch,
contract,
bend,
pull.

Be at once like a cat
and then a giraffe.

Roll up like a poly
and shift like a goalie.

Ask it to do force
then stretch what gripped.

Let it love like a purring kitty
and wallow like a pig in mud.

Your body knows,
your body's no.
Your body knows,
your body's yes.

Migraine

Vision blurs,
Tiny blip of sharp white light,
jagged little lightning bolt.

I prepare.
Won't be long
'til that lightning spreads,
flutters, pulses.

No need for psychedelics
with this brain.
Stressed lately
she steps in and says "enough".

This ocular aura,
light show in my eyes,
pops up on my mind screen
out of nowhere I know.

There was a time
it scared me.
I thought I was dying,
but didn't.

Dr. Man said
creative minds do it more.

Alice's own Wonderland,
came out of this mind madness,
where Lewis Carroll saw
necks stretch tall and bodies get small.

Dr. Man said
don't fight it,

lean in and let it teach you
like a magic trick
where the rabbit left the hat.

If I could show you this wildness I see
you'd just sit back and watch it with me.

Life, it's been full of itself lately.
My circuits tangled,
brain's tired so I stop.

This body,
the one I've loved on and abused,
given away 'til emptied of all fuel,
expanded, contracted,
she now leads,
teaches me every day.

Surrendered,
I wait out this lightning show with her
knowing she knows best.

Spirit

In that space between sleep and awakening,
I feel closest to you.
Dreamscapes took me in,
Gave me a world foreign and new.
Things unreal and real spoke to me
and I spoke to them.

My alarm plays Cristofori's dream.
I want to stay in psyche's playground.
Sadly, it's already gone.

Mom was there.
I needed an airline ticket home
and thought of flying with her.
The under bed was covered in old jewelry
as a dainty little bride in white floated
into the arms of her contracted future.

My eyes hold tight, I'm still here.
New day with you.

In the space between sleep and awakening
I sense your patience with me
as night scene quickly erases its dream.

You, still so close.
Today my feet don't eagerly slip from the bed
into uniform.
I linger here with eyes softened behind still
closed lids.

In this moment,
the one where choice after choice
will eventually define this day,
I inhale imagining you tethering me tight to you
before my feet touch the floor
and I forget I go it not alone.

Still in this space just after and before,
where softened eyes have yet to see this day,
I see you
seeing me
seeing you,
with love and hope for all this new day can become.

Bounties of Mutiny

Word Weaver
weave me a tale
of whimsy wild,
set free my sail.

Bounties of mutiny
stir deep within.
Away, sail away
let freedom begin.

Awaken my senses
Tune into their beat.
Rhythm's waves
turn up the heat.

Touch tickles
fickle fancies.
Sound subtly
disco dancing.

Smell sniffs
delights to devour.
Taste tempted
lips pucker sour.

Eyes soften,
spotting the way,
to feast upon life
throughout the day.

Rest, my Sweet, rest,
upon velvety rich dreams.
Behold your longings
are much closer than they seem.

All I Gotta Give

My all I gotta give
Is crunching, crashing, button-mashing,
blasting from my soul.
Bellowing, sunshiny yellowing saying to me,
Listen or I will hit you over your pretty head again.

My all I gotta give
still breathing, stopping, shaking.
Here ye, hear thee.
Breathe me in some real air,
more real than broken rattles,
shaken up between tired ears.

My all I gotta give
shines wickedly strong.
Pick up the pace
and squint through polarized eyes,
make out the shape of me
melting into goo...
imago knows clearly what we will become.

My all I gotta give
stirs words,
surfaces one clue.
Crazy eight ball says "yes" to questions not yet asked
waiting for you to suck deep roots up through fat feet,
waving arm limbs in breezes yet to blow.

My all I gotta give
wakes up,
looks down and laughs
cause it's simple,
uncomplicated,
unbound and free to roll on.

My all I gotta give
rolls over for free belly scratches
triggering right haunch wiggles,
because it just feels good.

My all I gotta give
soars because she can,
sleeps because she should,
and awakens on crisp sheets
cooled by stars retired from their eons work.

My all I gotta give
yells here I is and ain't I fine
'cause she listened,
and she learned,

and she has something to say
that matters.

No RSVP Required

I feel paused,
breathing deeper.

Breath held,
I'd walked underwater
overwhelmed in a world
I didn't choose
or did I?

My soul is an adventuer
who longs to throw open closed shutters
hiding the essence of my being.
The flame of my spirit held captive
too long by worlds too small,
where expansiveness felt vulnerable and alone.

This soul's been watered now –
the soil is richer
and more full of wild worms
and growing things that make me
tingle with excitement.

I long for words to flow on empty pages to tell you
stories of life sending postcards full of love to you
there watching from the sidelines,
while your life is on the field begging you to play.
I know you.
I am you.
I invite you in and on to live and breathe
just a little deeper.

Release

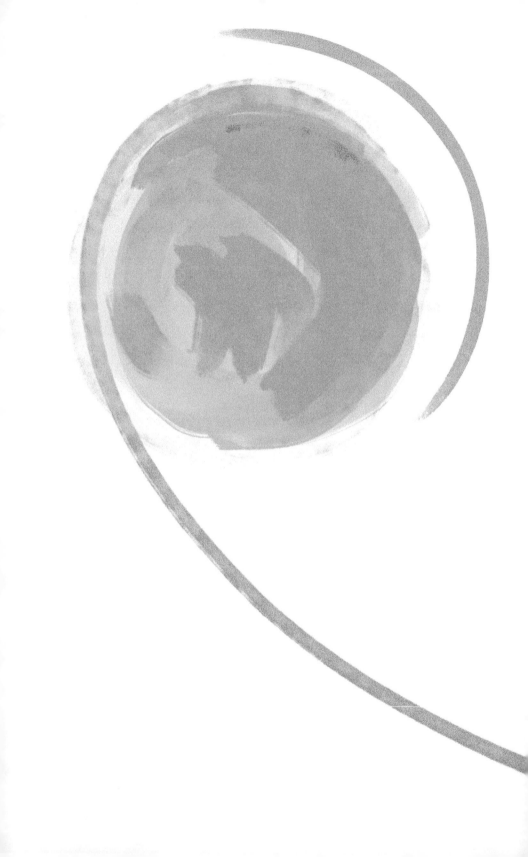

P.S.

A Soul That Sweet

Endings,
some timely,
some wanted,
some tragic,
some ever ending,
some never-ending,
some take breath away,
some crack it wide open and set it free.
This one, happened fast.

Love snuggled in my arms.
Eyes twitching.
Dreamland enchanted.
Little wiggles,
tiny grunts and sighs.
So warm.
Nestled against my heart.
I dared not move.

For I,
simply the holder of the dreamer,
held a miracle:
soon to take his last sleep,
soon to sigh his last sigh,
soon to close this short chapter.

In my limited human thinking,
I imagine him now small
cradled like a lost lamb
in our Shepherd's arms
but even that glorious image
feels too small.

On the evening his soul took leave,
I watched a little girl on a bike
and grieved all our little soul
would never do
when just then
she swerved towards me,
broke through my sadness,
looked me in my teary eyes
and hollered,
"Hello".

Just around the corner,
another little girl,
in a white party dress
ran through a garden of ivy.
Again sadness rose within me
until a big furry dog
broke free from its leash
and ran towards the girl.
Havoc. Laughter ensued.

Interrupted,
my train of thinking
didn't run me over.
Derailed,
I heard "set free"
the little girl joyfully on her bike,
the little girl deep to her knees in ivy,
the little soul here 60 days.

3 times he slept in my arms
each time resting against my heart.

His chest sharply rose
and fell with each breath.
Each time, I melted
like Irish butter left on the counter
softening for morning's fresh bake.

Time left,
didn't exist,
a soul that sweet,
an essence that pure,
living only under the influence of the Divine.
An angel before,
an angel in our arms,
an angel tasting a morsel of life
leaving behind his touch of grace.

Grief arrives.
sadness fills our tears,
as heart whispers,
"You've been touched by an angel."

How precious and rare it is,
to hold,
to be touched by,
to be in the presence of an angel,
mighty, willing, briefly gracing our world.

Written with much love and in memory of my nephew,
Barrett Calvin Fike
March 30 - May 28, 2021

Acknowledgements and Gratitude

With wholehearted thanks to…

-*You, Dear Reader*, for bringing *The Current* to life.

-*Art*, for always supporting and believing in my dreams.

-*Skyler*, you always inspire me to rise above, set a goal, and go for it. Your encouragement truly helped bring this book into being.

-*Adam*, you've helped me learn to better love adventures and move beyond my fears in ways I'd never imagined. Writing this book as you write yours has made this journey so much richer.

-*Fannie Belle Burnett (Mom)*, there would be no Current without you. Thank you for the feathers, lady bugs, and sleepy time whispers that kept me going and enchanted.

-*Sherry Burnett Watts*, because you never gave up on my dream to reach this moment and all the ones that will follow. Your confidence fueled my confidence and I'm forever grateful for this and all else.

-*Marilyn Burnett Williams*, my big jove buddy, you sat in the chair with me when nothing flowed, helped break the dam open wide, and always said just the right words all the way to the last line. You must be as relieved as I am that this puppy got born. Couldn't have done it without you.

-*Calvin Burnett*, for always being the rock when things get shaky, discovering I'm French, and telling tales that help me be more fascinating than I am.

-*Dr. Dan Watts*, you're the best writing playmate and most curious soul in the world. You help keep me flowing in mind, body, and spirit.

-*The rest of my amazing family*: Lynn, Mary Beth, Janice, Charlie, Elizabeth, Matt, Emmitt, Stacey, Dave, Connor, Ashlee, Ben, Kirra, Caleb, Danny, Fondren, Charlotte, Hudson, Nick, Dan, Carolyn, Robert, and our littlest angel, Barrett.

-*Brenda Stegall*, my voice of reason, friend for 55 years, and sassy fairy godmother.

-*Valentine Moulard Leonard*, this exists because of you, a poster, an email, a million prompts, a mermaid named Glow, an irreverent saucisson, and your belief that pigs do fly! Thank you seems way too small.

-*Hannah Kate Lewellen*, your artistic heart and immense creativity are true gifts. I'm honored to share the creative journey with you.

-*Michele Sammons*, your gifts helped set mine free. I'm forever grateful.

-*Eryn McEwan Seavey*, the little girls in white dresses frolicking by Walden Pond made the best soul pack ever!

-*Maureen Doyle*, 50 days apart, slapping loves around, and screaming Mother Mary, your Irish never backed down. Wouldn't have happened without you and Gymboree.

-Dr. Trish (all the rules broke when you arrived) Ring, for years of writing talks, the truth when most needed, "oh no she didn't say that" laughter, and your spirit full of generosity.

-Melissa Faber, for seeing what I wasn't seeing, nudging me past stuck places (like the back cover), and showing me how a southern writer best weaves words into magic.

-Pam Roth, for being *The Current*'s biggest cheerleader, listening day after day as each poem arrived, and being a constant reflection of "tethering tight".

-Dr. (Sister) Carole Riley, for naming the cracks and helping put Humpty Dumpty back together again with so much love.

-Signe Grushovenko, The Current's doula. Your artistry, friendship, and simpatico soul threw the doors to creativity and freedom wide open!

-Sarah Seidelmann, sessions with you in the fall of 2017 cracked the door open that first shined light upon *The Current* to come.

-Lisa Sanchez Sullivan, your 5am then 6am sass and "you can do it" continue to wake up my life in every way.

-Cindy Westcott, supporting me and all as only the sunflower girl would do.

-Lisa Holt, for always being there at just the right time and joyfully looking through *The Current*'s galleys with me

-Shelley Vogel, for being the eternal cheerleader for all the best life can bring.

-Lynn Eisenstatt, for being a safe place to land when the waters toss and the most innovative person I know.

-Dearest friends who've believed and encouraged me to write, I'm honored to share life's journey with you Jill Micai, Anna Esquivel, Robin Marberry Casey, Angel Auricchio, Mae Jensen, Mike Falcone,

Jennifer Poyner, Leslie Schutt, Mary Fortin, Jeanne Simmons.
-*The Interesting Women's Book Club*, 22 years of listening, waiting, and encouraging. Mary Beth, thank you for taking care of the IWBC and keeping so much creativity and hope around me for all of these years.

-*The Memphis Writer's Ensemble*, all of you and your wild creativity.

-*St. Clare Silent Retreats*, where silence and sacred inspiration always emerge.

-*The Rev. Mimsy Jones*, your enthusiasm, big smile, true delight, and say it how it is honesty help keep me young and growing.

-*St. Columba Episcopal Camp and Retreat Center*, poetry's ideal backdrop.

-*Soul Circle friends*, Maureen McGargill, Christine Broughton, and Laura Carpenter encouraging me these past months to get to this finish line.

-*The Rev. Sandy Webb*, for our sincere conversations.

-*Susan Austin Crumpton*, for teaching me how big and beautiful love can be. Wise counselor, Earth Mother, you are the bearer of possibility.

-*Belleanny Hope and the Muses*.

-*The Mississippi River and Downtown Memphis*, for always inspiring me.

-*Imagination*, where all is possible.

-*My creativity*, you remembered.

About the Author and Illustrator

Connie Cruthirds, *author*

Connie Cruthirds, storyteller, photo-journeyist, and a weaver of words in the style of Mary Oliver and David Whyte, writes to discover the intriguing life within us all. Much like her supposed cousin, Mark Twain, Connie lives on a bluff by the Mississippi River, where the currents of life lap past her door. She is married, with two  adult children, and is a creative coach helping people find their way through life. Connie's work has been featured in *Beyond Knowing, Huffington Post, A Sacred Presence, Lifeline, and Mais Oui* I, II, and III.

For more about Connie and her work visit her website: **www.conniecruthirds.com**

Hannah Kate Lewellen, *illustrator*

Hannah Kate Lewellen is an artist and illustrator whose work ranges from commissioned paintings for individuals to larger installation pieces that she creates for the local children's hospital. She is happiest painting landscapes and creating pieces that echo the beauty of the outdoors and allow the viewer a moment of escape and tranquility.

Bringing these small moments of peace into other people's spaces is an honor for Hannah, whether it's the walls of a home or the halls of a hospital. She believes that creative expression can play a powerful role in healing, learning, and processing. She has seen these therapeutic benefits in her own life through her art making process which led her to pursue her work at the intersection of arts and medicine/healthcare.

For more about Hannah and her work visit her website: **www.hkate.com**

CPSIA information can be obtained
at www.ICGtesting.com
Printed in the USA
LVHW011030211121
703847LV00001B/3